Sewing Bits & Pieces

35 Projects Using Fabric Scraps

Sandi Henderson

WILEY

Wiley Publishing, Inc.

Credits

Acquisitions Editor
Roxane Cerda

Project Editor
Lynn Northrup

Editorial Manager
Christina Stambaugh

Publisher
Cindy Kitchel

**Vice President and
Executive Publisher**
Kathy Nebenhaus

Interior Design
Erin Zeltner

Graphics
Brooke Graczyk
Brent Savage

Photography
Sandi Henderson

Library of Congress Cataloging-in-Publication Data:
Henderson, Sandi.
 Sewing bits and pieces : 35 projects using fabric scraps / Sandi Henderson.
    p. cm.
 ISBN-13: 978-0-470-53924-8
 ISBN-10: 0-470-53924-0
 1. Sewing. 2. Textiles fabrics. I. Title.
 TT705.H46 2010
 646.2--dc22
                                2010002934

Printed in the United States of America

10 9 8 7 6 5 4 3 2

Book production by Wiley Publishing, Inc., Composition Services

Sandi's original patterns are intended for non-commercial, personal use only and may not be used in the production of goods for sale in any quantity.

Acknowledgments

To my husband Dustin, without whom I would not be the person I am today. My dreams would not have reached so far, my desires would not have been so fulfilled, and my home would not be filled with so much laughter. Thank you for being the most supportive husband and best father I have ever encountered. Thank you for taking me on a date every Friday night and for rubbing my feet every time I want it but don't ask for it. You are THE best.

To my sweet first-born Eliza, thank you for making me smile every day with your love of dinosaurs and brilliant knack for drawing at the ripe old age of five. You were the reason I started my business, and you bring me more inspiration than I can keep up with on a daily basis.

To my spritely and happy Ethan, thank you for filling our home with laughter and weird sounds. Many of the projects in this book were inspired by you and your innocent little-boy spirit; I so wanted to share that with others.

Thank you to my friends and family for supporting me in all of my endeavors, which are not always simple. The inner peace that comes from knowing my family is proud of me is something that can never quite be described in writing.

Thank you to the people who read my silly little blog—the joy that I get from sharing my words, fabrics, and projects with you is overwhelming. Even if we have never had personal contact, if you have been to my blog, I consider you my friend.

Thank you to Wiley Publishing for entrusting me with the task of bringing this book to fruition; it has been a joy.

Thank you to Michael Miller Fabrics for being the first company to give me a shot at something big and for providing me with mountains and mountains of fabric.

Thank you to Moda Fabrics and Free Spirit Fabrics for providing me with nice fat stacks of several fabric collections I wanted to include in my book.

Table of Contents

Foreword

When Sandi asked me to write the foreword for this book, besides being honored and flattered, it triggered memories of our first meeting at the International Quilt Market in spring 2007.

There she was at our booth, portfolio in hand; after an introduction, we had the typical sit-down and "let's see what you've got." Her designs and color sense were fresh and wonderful, but what really struck me was her "being." There was a calmness in her belief in herself and a generosity of spirit that inspires trust—the trust necessary to form a bond between an art director and artist. I knew she was the "real deal" and shared her belief that the time was right for the next step in her creative journey.

Her fabric collections—Ginger Blossom, Farmers Market, and Meadowsweet—have wowed us all. Her sewing patterns, blog, and now, this delightful book, take us along with her, inspiring us all in our creative journeys.

Kathy Miller

Co-President, Michael Miller Fabrics

Introduction

Fabric.

Oh, how we love it! What is it about that chunky stack of freshly cut cotton that drives us to giddy happiness? I think it's the potential behind it; the many projects that you could create with that pretty new bundle. That fabric could become a new bag, skirt, tablecloth, or pillows for your living room. Just thinking about it makes me want to run to my fabric cupboard and start taking out stacks to play with the combinations.

However, after we decide on the perfect project and bring it to fruition, we are undoubtedly left with the remnants of the project: scraps. It's a word I don't care for, actually. It sounds like something you wouldn't want around. But the fabric remnants from my beloved projects are just as cherished as the larger pieces! They are still beautiful and they still have potential. I don't use fabric I don't love, so why would a smaller piece be any less special?

But I see it all the time—people get stumped on what to do with all those scraps. When the idea of this book was brought to me, I knew it was the right project for me to take on. What has resulted is a collection of projects that I am proud to send out into the world. I love using what is around before buying more. I enjoy buying that new yardage so much more when I know I used the last of it to its full potential!

Here are a few things to keep in mind when working on projects in this book:

- Your scraps will most likely come from different projects. Make sure that the care is the same on each fabric you combine in a project, such as prewashing for shrinkage.
- Most of the fabrics I use in this book are quilting-weight cottons, but you could use a wide range of weights for the projects. Just take care to only combine fabrics that have a similar stretch to them. For example, feel free to mix cottons with cords, but I wouldn't recommend combining knits with velvets unless it happens to be stretch velvet.
- If you are just starting out sewing and don't have a scrap pile waiting to be busted into, that's okay! Many fabric manufacturers offer convenient precuts of fabric that are perfect for many of the projects in this book. Most independent quilt shops carry them as well as online suppliers. I offer an extensive list of retailers on my Web site: www.sandihendersondesign.com.

I hope you enjoy the projects in this book as much as I enjoyed putting them together. What I found most satisfying about the projects I made for this book was the story they told. Little bits and pieces of different projects found their way into new ones and there was a connecting thread. Just as purchasing a new sweater while on vacation brings memories of your vacation each time you wear it, using fabrics left over from beloved sewing projects brings a new layer of memories to a handcrafted item. I hope you will experience the same joy when you create something special for someone you love from your own bits and pieces.

Enjoy!

Commonly Used Sewing Terms

Here are some terms I use frequently throughout the book:

- **binding:** This is a fabric-encased edging for projects. Binding can be made or purchased. This book has projects that use both bias binding (Hanging Organizer, Picnic Quilt) and straight-cut fabric-encased binding (Birthday Party Garland, Fruit Appliqué Tablecloth).

- **edge stitch:** This is a finishing stitch sewn approximately ⅛″ away from a joining hem on the right side of the fabric.

- **French knot:** This decorative embroidery stitch results in a neat little knot. It can be used for a decorative little pop of color almost anywhere. Push the needle through the fabric from the wrong side. Wrap the thread two or three times around the needle, keeping the thread taut, and gently push the needle back through the fabric very close to where it came out. You can gently tighten the stitch by pulling the thread from below. This stitch is used in the Cherry Blossom Tee, Forest Owl, Herbal Sachet, and Upscaled Cardigan projects.

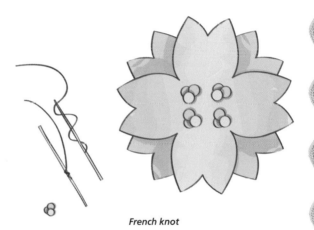

French knot

- **gather:** Gathering is used to create a ruffle. There are two good ways to do this. The method I use most of the time is to create a long spaced stitch with my sewing machine and gently pull one thread to gather the fabric. If you are gathering heavier layers, sew a zigzag stitch over a piece of heavy thread or floss. Pull the heavy thread or floss to gather.

- **machine appliqué:** I mention machine appliqué in several projects in the book, such as the Bubbly Shower Curtain, Forest Owl, Garden Pillows, Scrappy Silhouettes, Story Time Quilt, and Woodland Bunny. This is a simple process that is basically sewing an appliqué piece down with your sewing machine. I usually choose a monofilament (clear) thread and a small zigzag stitch and overlap the edge of the appliqué shapes with the zigzags.

- **rolled hem:** A rolled hem is done on a serger and is the perfect finishing edge for ruffles (Colorful Brick Road Skirt) or peasant top necklines and sleeves. If you don't have a serger, I give alternate instructions where this step is called for, but I love the finished touch it gives. (If you plan on sewing a lot of garments, definitely put a serger on your birthday wish list!)

- **running stitch:** This simple embroidery stitch is done by pushing the needle up and down through the fabric, leaving a small space between each stitch. This is used as the quilting method

Running stitch

for the Story Time Quilt and can be added to different projects for a pop of color and interest.

- ⚙ **stay stitch:** This is a basting stitch that is used as a placeholder; it is not intended to hold the fabric permanently.

- ⚙ **whip stitch:** This hand-sewn stitch is used for finishing edges or joining two pieces of fabric. Working approximately ¼" from the edge, insert the needle through the wrong side of the fabric(s) from bottom to top. "Whip" it around the edge of the fabric and insert the needle again from bottom to

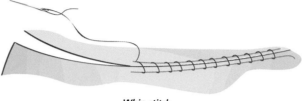

Whip stitch

top one stitch length from the last stitch. This stitch is used for several projects in this book, such as the Dahlia Pincushion, Forest Owl, Hanging Organizer, Mary Jane Slippers, Picnic Quilt, Story Time Quilt, and Woodland Bunny.

Commonly Used Tools

Every great cook works with good tools and great ingredients. If you want to be a great seamstress, the same theory applies! Allow yourself quality materials and tools, and your end result will be better. End of story. Here are some common tools I mention in this book:

- ⚙ **adhesive:** I use two types of craft adhesives interchangeably. Spray adhesive comes in an aerosol can and can be sprayed on. I also use decoupage medium as a brush-on glue and sealer. Spray adhesive and decoupage medium can be used together, and they can usually be used interchangeably. However, spray adhesive should not be used as a sealer, because it will dry tacky.

- ⚙ **buttons and trims:** I have a metal tin full of buttons in all shapes and sizes and will sometimes sort through it just to enjoy the collection I'm working on. Trims are the same story. I have a variety of crochet trims, lace, and various embroidered borders. Finishing a project with the right trims is like picking out the perfect earrings and shoes to go with an outfit.

- ⚙ **cotton tee shirts:** These are great for embellishing with scraps. Wash them first to preshrink them.

- ⚙ **double-sided iron-on adhesive:** I use this for appliqué. You buy it off a bolt and it comes with a paper backing. You place the adhesive side on the wrong side of your fabric and iron. Cut out your desired shape, peel the paper backing off of the adhesive, and place onto another piece of fabric, tacky side down. Iron in place.

- ⚙ **elastic:** Unless I am sewing with especially dark fabric, I always use white elastic. Regardless of the color of fabric you are using, the white won't show through. For darker fabrics, there is also black elastic.

- ⚙ **fabric-covered buttons:** This is one of my favorite ways to use up scrap fabrics. You can find the kits in the notions section of the fabric store.

- **fusible batting:** Lightweight batting that is fusible to fabric on one side. You can purchase this by the yard.
- **hook & loop tape:** Known most commonly as the brand Velcro, this product has a prickly side and a soft side (known as male and female) and adheres to its opposite part. I used hook & loop tape for the Countdown Chain.
- **lightweight fusible interfacing:** This is different from double-sided adhesive as it is only fusible on one side and is used to provide stability and weight to a project.
- **needle and embroidery floss:** Keep a candy-coated library of embroidery floss on hand. They are inexpensive and will make you happy.
- **pins:** Collect a few different types. My favorites are quilting pins. They are long and skinny and I use them for almost all projects. I also have some thicker pins that work better for heavier fabrics such as denim.
- **quilt batting:** Just like everything, this comes in different qualities. If you are going to go to the time and effort of making a quilt, do yourself a favor and use the best batting. I like wool batting because it's thin but oh-so-warm, and it provides that pretty crinkle that I love quilts to get after they are washed for the first time.
- **scissors:** Do yourself a favor and invest in a really good pair. You won't regret it, and they last forever! My favorites are my Ginghers. I bought them one day years ago with a 40 percent off coupon and some babysitting money I had saved up. I still have them and use them almost every day.
- **serger:** I don't sew any clothing without using my serger. It creates a professional finish and opens up a world of options you don't have with a sewing machine alone. Different from sewing machines, sergers have the ability to cut away excess fabric as you are sewing and finish the seam so it is very tidy.
- **sewing machine:** Many of these projects are easily accomplished by hand-sewing alone, but a good sewing machine will create tighter stitches and a stronger hem. Surprisingly, this is the one tool that I don't suggest going all out on. You can get a very good sewing machine that will do the job for a much smaller price than the top-of-the-line models run. I'm a huge advocate of buying something to last, however, so look at your needs and do your research. Find a model that performs the stitches and functions you will use, and will do them well.
- **spray starch:** Spray starch comes in an aerosol can and is just what it sounds like. You spray the starch on the fabric and iron to get a nice crisp finish. I use this to form the shapes in both of my quilts in this book (Picnic Quilt and Story Time Quilt) but I also use it every time I iron a garment I have made by hand.
- **wool felt:** I collect wool felt like I do fabric. You can find different blends, but my favorite is good old 100 percent wool. Bamboo blends are silky to the touch and quite fun to use also. All of the projects in this book that call for wool felt (Dahlia Pincushion, Forest Owl, Garden Pillows, Herbal Sachet, Fruit Appliqué Tablecloth, Upscaled Cardigan, and Woodland Bunny) were made using 100 percent wool felt.
- **wool or polyester fiberfill:** This is the filling of choice for projects that are stuffed, such as the Dahlia Pincushion or Forest Owl. I prefer wool, which stuffs easier and molds a project better. But polyester fiberfill is much more economical and works well, too.

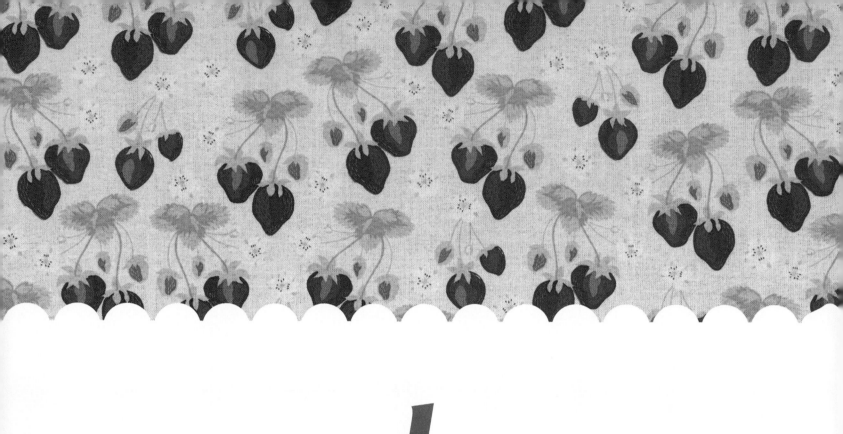

1

Kitchen

Fruit Appliqué Tablecloth

Fruit Appliqué Tablecloth

This is the perfect project for using extra-special scraps. While once attending the International Quilt Market, I walked past a vintage fabric booth and found, to my delight, a little bag of some of the loveliest fabric I'd ever seen. I saved it for a long time, waiting for the perfect project to come to mind. This tablecloth fit the bill! I finished my edges with the Patchwork Edge Trim from page 124. Since the Patchwork Edge Trim is not cut on the bias, I have written the instructions for this project without continuous binding on the corners. You could certainly substitute true bias tape for the edges and create continuous binding with mitered corners. (View the binding steps on either the Picnic Quilt on page 126 or the Hanging Organizer on page 29 for reference.)

Supplies

Fabric scraps—between 2" and 8" in size

For each apple:
   1 piece of fabric for the apple, 5½" × 6"
   1 piece of wool felt or fabric for the leaf, 1" × 2"
   1 piece of wool felt or fabric for the stem, 1½" × 1"

For each cherry:
   1 piece of fabric for the cherry, 2" × 2"
   1 piece of wool felt or fabric for the leaf, 1" × 1½"

For each orange:
   1 piece of fabric for the orange, 3" × 2½"
   1 piece of wool felt or fabric for the stem, 2½" × 1"

For each pear:
   1 piece of fabric for the pear, 3½" × 4½"
   1 piece of wool felt or fabric for the leaf, 2½" × 2"

For each strawberry:
   1 piece of fabric for the strawberry, 3" × 3"
   1 piece of wool felt or fabric for the leaf, 2½" × 1"
   1 sliver of wool felt for the stem

Vellum or tracing paper

Double-sided iron-on adhesive

1 solid-colored tablecloth to fit your table

Patchwork Edge Trim (see page 124): 2 pieces the length of your tablecloth and 2 pieces the width of your tablecloth; or, if you are using a round tablecloth, enough 1" double-fold bias tape to go around the edge

Note: I don't recommend the Patchwork Edge Trim for a round tablecloth as it is not a true bias tape and will most likely pucker around the curves.

Prep

1 Prepare your tablecloth. If you are buying a new tablecloth, wash, dry, and press it. Cut off the finished edges.

Note: If you can't find a new tablecloth in the shape or color you want, you can craft one from a bedsheet. Measure your table and allow 12" of overhang on each side. Trim to the correct size, but don't hem the edges.

2 Trace the pattern pieces for the fruit shapes on pages 157–158 by layering vellum or tracing paper over the page and lightly tracing the pattern with a pencil. (There are three sizes of each

fruit shape; for this project you will use the medium shape only.) Remove the tracing paper from the book and darken your line with a marker.

Creating the Fruit Appliqués

3 Adhere double-sided adhesive to the wrong side of your fabric scraps. Cut your fruit pieces out of the fabric. The number of fruit pieces you will need depends on how large your tablecloth is and how you want to space the pieces. Start with four or five of each shape.

4 Decide on the placement of your fruit pieces. I placed mine about 4" from the edge around the border of the tablecloth. Then, one at a time, peel the paper backing off the pieces and iron them in place. Sew the fruit shapes to the tablecloth with monofilament thread. I like to use a small zigzag stitch around the edge to do this.

Step 4

5 Continue sewing fruit shapes to the tablecloth until you have the desired number in place. Add any leaves or stems to the fruit.

Attaching the Binding

6 Unfold one of your binding strips. With the wrong side facing you, pin the raw edge of the strip to the raw edge of the wrong side of your tablecloth. Sew along the first fold line.

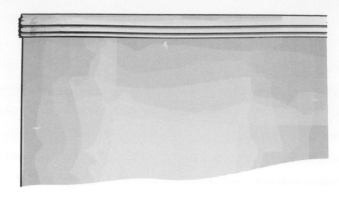

Step 6

7 Fold the strip over to the front side of the tablecloth. Pin in place and stitch along the folded edge. Repeat Steps 6 and 7 for the opposite side of the tablecloth.

Step 7

8 Repeat Steps 6 and 7 for the edges you haven't finished yet. At the edges, fold the strip wrong side in about an inch before sewing it in place.

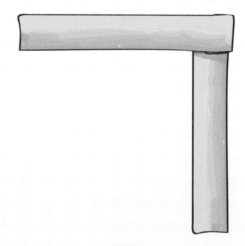

Step 8

9 Press and enjoy!

Sweet Treats Towels

Sweet Treats Towels

Whip up a handful of these appliqué towels on a lazy Saturday. They'll bring you just as much joy as the treats you cool on them. I've used linen for my towels, but muslin, cotton, or even a recycled bedsheet will work wonderfully!

Supplies

For one towel, one 24" × 36" piece of solid, prewashed fabric

For each cupcake appliqué:
   1 fabric scrap for the cupcake rim (brown for chocolate, cream for vanilla, pink for strawberry), 6" × 2"
   1 fabric scrap for the frosted cupcake top, 6" × 4"
   1 fabric scrap for the cupcake base (stripes are fun for this!), 5" × 3"
   1 fabric scrap for the cherry, 2" × 2"
   1 fabric scrap for the leaf, 1" × 2"

For each ice cream sundae appliqué:
   Fabric scraps in three different fabrics for the ice cream balls, 4" × 4"
   1 fabric scrap for the dish, 6" × 5"
   1 fabric scrap for the whipped cream, 3" × 3"

For each pie appliqué:
   1 fabric scrap for the pie top (I show a brown crust top, but try a fruit-colored one), 10" × 3"
   1 fabric scrap for the base, 9" × 3"
   1 fabric scrap for the steamy goodness, 2" × 3"

Vellum or tracing paper

Double-sided iron-on fabric adhesive for each piece of appliqué fabric

Needle and embroidery floss, or sewing machine to appliqué with

Embellishments (optional)

Prep

1 Cut your towel piece out of prewashed fabric.

2 Trace the appliqué pattern pieces for the cupcake, ice cream sundae, or pie shapes as needed (see pages 159–160) by layering vellum or tracing paper over the page and lightly tracing the pattern with a pencil. Iron the double-sided fabric adhesive onto the wrong side of your fabric pieces for the appliqué according to the manufacturer's instructions.

Appliqué

3 Peel the paper backing off of the appliqué pieces. Iron the appliqué pieces onto your towel in the order given on the next page and stitch each one in place before moving on to the next piece.

Note: You can use a straight stitch or satin stitch on your sewing machine, or any number of fun embroidery stitches with a needle and embroidery floss. Since this is a small project, it's a great place to experiment with embroidery, even if you've never done it before!

For the cupcake: Begin with the base, then the cupcake rim, then the frosting top, followed by the cherry and leaf.

For the pie: Start with the pie plate, then the pie top, then the steam.

For the ice cream sundae: Layer the three ice cream scoops first, sewing each one before adding the next. Add the whipped cream and the dish.

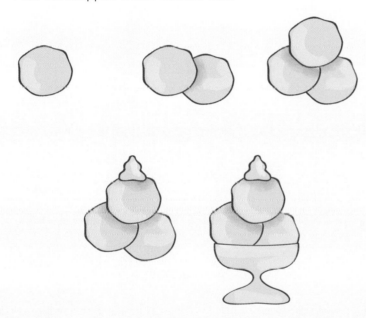

Finishing

4 Press the long sides of the towel ¼" to the wrong side of the towel. Turn and press another ¼". Stitch along the folded edge. Repeat with the short ends of the towel.

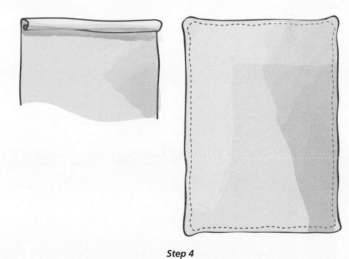

Step 4

5 Sew on or embroider any embellishments you would like. Rickrack on the sides adds a nice retro touch.

Fruit Magnets

Fruit Magnets

Does your refrigerator play host to artwork, photos, and report cards? It can become a bit of a jumble! Whip up a collection of these sweet magnets to help showcase that memorabilia in a neat and tidy manner. The added cute factor doesn't hurt, either.

Supplies

For the apple:
  1 fabric scrap for the outside, 5½" × 6"
  1 piece of very stiff interfacing, 5½" × 6"
  1 piece of wool felt for the back, 5" × 5"
  1 piece of wool felt for the leaf, 1" × 2"
  1 piece of wool felt for the stem, 1½" × 1"

For the cherry:
  1 fabric scrap for the outside, 2½" × 2½"
  1 piece of very stiff interfacing, 2" × 2"
  1 piece of wool felt for the back, 2" × 2"
  1 piece of wool felt for the leaf, 1" × 1½"

For the orange:
  1 fabric scrap for the outside, 4" × 3½"
  1 piece of very stiff interfacing, 3" × 2½"
  1 piece of wool felt for the back, 3" × 2½"
  1 piece of wool felt for the stem, 2½" × 1"

For the pear:
  1 fabric scrap for the outside, 4" × 5½"
  1 piece of very stiff interfacing, 3½" × 4½"
  1 piece of wool felt for the back, 3½" ×4½"
  1 piece of wool felt for the leaf, 2½" × 2"

For the strawberry:
  1 fabric scrap for the outside, 3½" × 4"
  1 piece of very stiff interfacing, 3" × 3"
  1 piece of wool felt for the back, 3" × 3"
  1 piece of wool felt for the leaves, 1½" × 1"
  1 sliver of wool felt for the stem

Vellum or tracing paper

Double-sided iron-on fabric adhesive

Needle and embroidery floss

Parchment paper

Hot glue gun

Plain magnets

Trims such as buttons or crocheted flowers (optional)

Prep

1 Trace the pattern pieces on pages 157–158 for the fruit magnets you wish to make by layering vellum or tracing paper over the page and lightly tracing the pattern with a pencil. There are three sizes of each shape: The largest size is for the fabric, the middle size is for the interfacing, and the smallest size is for the wool felt backing.

Creating the Fruit Body

2 Adhere double-sided adhesive to the wrong side of your fabric. Cut the largest pattern piece out of the fabric.

3 Cut the middle-sized pattern piece out of the stiff interfacing. Place the interfacing shape down on a larger piece of parchment paper. Peel the paper lining off of the double-sided adhesive on the fabric fruit piece. Place the fabric fruit piece right side up on top of the interfacing piece, arranging it so you have an overlap of about ½" on all sides. Lightly iron the fabric in place to adhere it to the interfacing. The interfacing will melt; allow it to cool and then gently peel it off of the parchment paper.

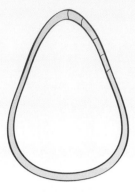

Step 4

5 Turn the edges of the fabric to the back of the interfacing, ironing them in place one at a time.

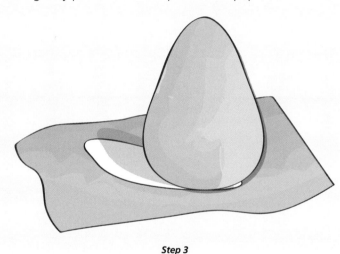

Step 3

4 Clip the edges of the fabric, spacing about ¾" apart.

Step 5

Finishing

6 With a needle and embroidery floss (I recommend using three threads), do a running stitch around the border of your fruit. If you wish, you can add seeds or other embroidered embellishments.

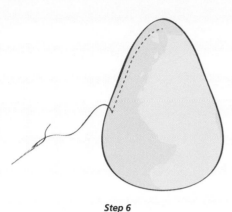

Step 6

7 Adhere double-sided adhesive to a piece of wool felt. Cut out the smallest size pattern piece out of the felt. Peel the paper lining off of the adhesive and place this side against the interfacing side of the fruit body. Iron in place.

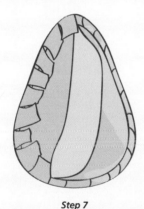

Step 7

8 Cut out the stems and leaves for your fruit and adhere them in place using a hot glue gun. If you like, add trims or flowers to the stems for extra pop.

Step 8

9 Using your hot glue gun, adhere a magnet to the back side of the fruit body.

Note: There are many different sizes and shapes of magnets available; I always keep several different kinds on hand. You can usually find plain magnets near the beads in craft stores.

Foodie Bags

Foodie Bags

In my earth-loving, hippie town, we have an amazing natural grocery store with rows and rows of bulk food choices. I love shopping there, and wanted to create some reusable bags that I could take with me. I chose breathable linen for the body of the bag, and added a bright strip of fabric for interest. This makes a perfect scrap project—and it's environmentally friendly, too. I haven't been to the grocery store once with these bags without people asking where they can get one!

Supplies

For the wide bag:
  1 piece of fabric, 8" × 28"
  1 contrasting strip of fabric, 8" × 1½"
  1 piece of double-sided iron-on adhesive, 8" × 1½"
  1 12" piece of ribbon, twine, or bias tape that has been sewn shut

For the narrow bag:
  1 piece of fabric, 10" × 22"
  1 contrasting strip of fabric, 10" × 1½"
  1 piece of double-sided iron-on adhesive, 10" × 1½"
  1 14" piece of ribbon, twine, or bias tape that has been sewn shut

Prep

1 Make sure all fabrics are prewashed and ironed. Cut out all pieces.

Creating the Contrast Strip

2 Iron the double-sided adhesive on to the wrong side of your contrasting strip.

3 Peel the paper lining off of the back and place the strip on the right side of your bag fabric, 5" from the top. Press in place, then edge-stitch along both long edges.

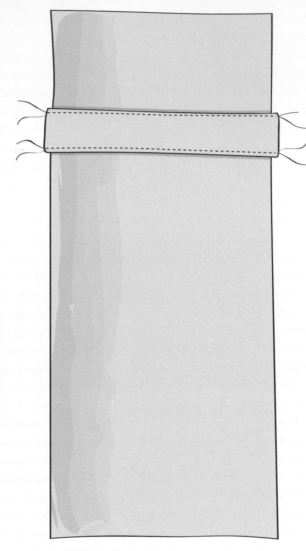

Step 3

Forming the Bag

4 You will be making French seams, so you'll sew first on the right side. Fold the bag in half, wrong sides together, and sew the side seams with a tight stitch. Trim away the excess material as close to the seam as you can.

Step 4

Creating the Gussets

5 Fold the bag so the side seams are centered on the top and bottom, running down to a point. Measure 1" from the tip of each corner and cut perpendicular to the side seam. Pin the opening you have made in place. Cut and pin the other corner in the same way, then sew each corner shut. Trim away as much of the excess fabric as possible.

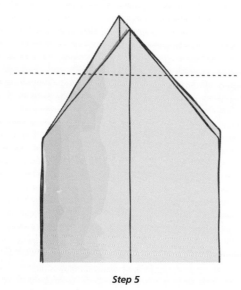

Step 5

Making the French Seams

6 Turn the bag wrong side out and press. Sew the side seams first and then the gusset seams to encase them. Turn the bag right side out.

Finishing

7 On the right side of the bag, make two ½" buttonholes on either side of one side seam, starting 1½" from the top of the bag.

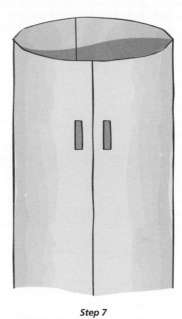

Step 7

8 Fold the top edge ½" over to the wrong side of the bag. Press.

9 Fold 1" more, press, and pin in place. Sew the casing shut with a ¼" seam allowance along the folded edge.

10 Using a safety pin as a guide, insert your drawstring of choice into the casing through one of the buttonholes and thread it through the casing and out the opposite buttonhole.

2

Bed & Bath

Patchwork Pillow

Patchwork Pillow

Next to painting a wall, new pillows are the best way to add some pop to your home. This particular pillow adds a handcrafted touch that I love. Your home is a haven, a place for your family to retreat at the end of the day. Take the time to make it your own. This pillow resides on my son's bed—I love that every time he looks at it, he knows that he is important enough to have a handcrafted item all his own.

Supplies

12 strips of fabric, each 3¼" × 10"

8 strips of fabric, each 3¼" × 5½"

2 pieces of fabric for the back, each 15" × 19"

2 pieces of fusible lightweight interfacing for the back, each 15" × 19"

1 piece of double-sided iron-on adhesive, 19" × 19"

1 piece of muslin, 19" × 19"

1 18" pillow form

Prep

1   Cut all strips and back pieces.

Creating the Strips

2   Place two of your 3¼" × 10" strips right sides together and sew at the short end using a ½" seam allowance. Press the seam open. Repeat with six other strips to create a total of four strips, each 3¼" × 19".

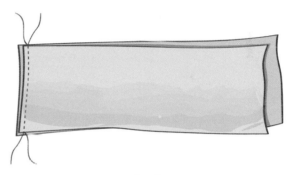

Step 2

3   Place one 3¼" × 10" strip right sides together to one 3¼" × 5½" strip. Sew together at the short end. Press the seam open. Repeat on the opposite side of the strip with a coordinating 3¼" × 5½" piece. Press the seam open. Repeat to create a total of four strips, each 3¼" × 19".

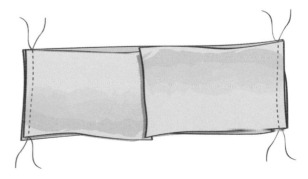

Step 3

Forming the Front

4 Sew your strips right sides together along the long sides, alternating the two-strip and three-strip sections.

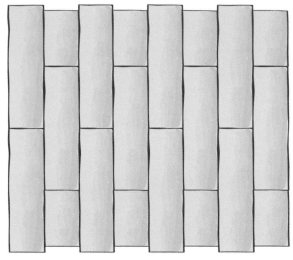

Step 4

5 Trim the top so that it is a perfect 19" × 19" square.

6 Iron on the double-sided adhesive to the wrong side of your pillow front. Peel the paper backing away and lay the wrong side on the muslin. Press together. This will make your pillow front much more durable.

7 Topstitch straight lines ¼" from each of your seams on the pillow front.

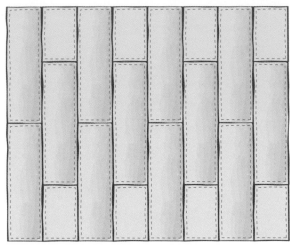

Step 7

Forming the Pillow Back

8 Press the iron-on interfacing to the wrong side of each of your back pillow pieces.

9 On one back piece, fold one of the 19" sides 1½" to the wrong side. Press. Repeat with the other back piece.

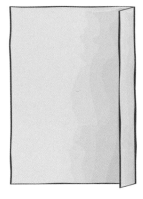

Step 9

10 Fold under again another 1½", press, and stitch along the folded edge. Repeat with the other back piece.

Step 10

11 Place one of the pillow back pieces over the top of the other and align so they make a 19" × 19" square. Sew together at the top and the bottom.

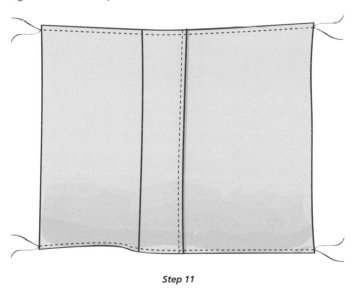

Step 11

Finishing

12 Place the pillow front right sides together to the pillow back. Trim any edges if needed. Sew together around all sides. Turn right side out through the opening in the back. Insert your pillow form.

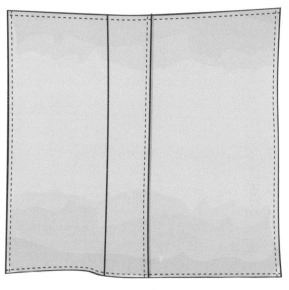

Step 12

Hanging Organizer

Hanging Organizer

Both of my children have one of these handy organizers by their bed. It's the perfect catchall for books, toys, flashlights, and water bottles. They also love to use these organizers as their own mailboxes to tuck away drawings and notes to each other.

Supplies

2 pieces of linen or solid-colored fabric for the front and back, each 20" × 38"

2 pieces of fusible batting, each 20" × 38"

1 piece of double-sided adhesive, 20" × 38"

1 package of ½" wide double-fold bias tape

1 package of 1" wide double-fold bias tape

4 fabric pieces for the small pockets, each 9" × 17"

4 pieces of lightweight fusible interfacing for the small pockets, each 9" × 17"

1 fabric piece for the large pocket, 18" × 16"

1 piece of lightweight fusible interfacing for the large pocket, 18" × 16"

1 6" length of grosgrain ribbon, ⅞" wide

1 10" length of grosgrain ribbon, ⅞" wide

3 grommets and grommet tool

Prep

1 Cut out all pieces.

Creating the Front and Back

2 Fuse one 20" wide × 38" long piece of batting to the wrong side of your linen front. Trim to 18" wide × 36" long. Repeat with the back. Set aside the back piece for now.

Creating the Pockets

3 Fuse the lightweight interfacing to the wrong side of each pocket piece. Fold each pocket in half, matching the 9" ends right sides together, and sew along the two sides. Turn right side out and press.

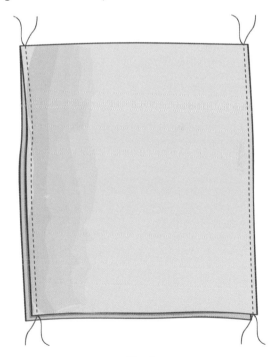

Step 3

4 Press the pocket flat. Edge-stitch around all four sides of each pocket.

Step 4

Step 5

Creating the Pleat

5 Find the center point of one of the pockets by folding it in half. Make a small pencil mark at the center of the pocket on the bottom edge. Repeat with the remaining pockets.

6 Fold each bottom corner of your pocket to the center mark. Pin in place and press. Make a new small pencil mark on each fold. Unfold each pocket.

7 Fold the outer pencil marks to the inside pencil mark. Pin in place at the top and bottom of the pocket. Press and baste along the bottom of the pocket. Repeat with the remaining pockets.

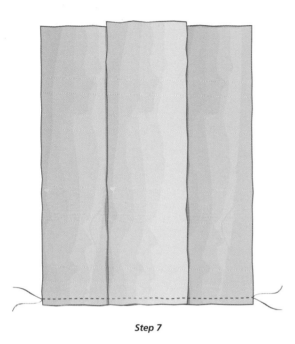

Step 7

8 Cut four lengths of ½" bias tape, each slightly longer than the width of your pocket. Unfold the side of the bias tape that is slightly shorter than the other. Pin the raw edge of the bias tape to the wrong side of the bottom edge of the pocket. Sew along the fold of the bias tape. Repeat with the remaining pockets.

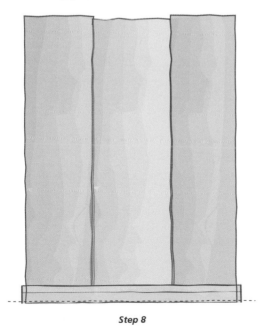

Step 8

9 Fold the bias tape to the right side of the pocket. Tuck the raw edge of the tape to the back of the pocket. Pin in place. Repeat with the remaining pockets.

Attaching the Pockets

10 Pin your pockets to the organizer front piece as shown.

Step 10

11 Sew the pockets to the organizer front. Start with the bottom edge. Sew around the four sides of the bias tape. Then sew the sides of the pocket in place, being sure to backstitch at the top of the pocket.

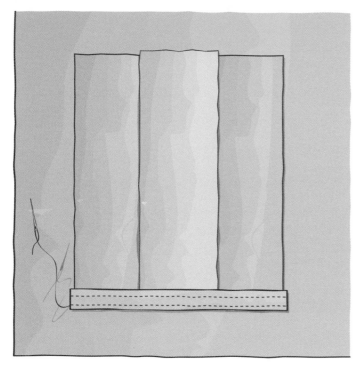

Step 11

12 Fold the edges of your ribbon strips under to the wrong side and pin in place. (Don't heat with the iron; this will melt most ribbons!) Pin to the front of the organizer and sew in place at the sides. If you plan on using the ribbon holders for pens, scissors, and so on, sew a few stitches at different sections of your ribbon strip to help support individual items.

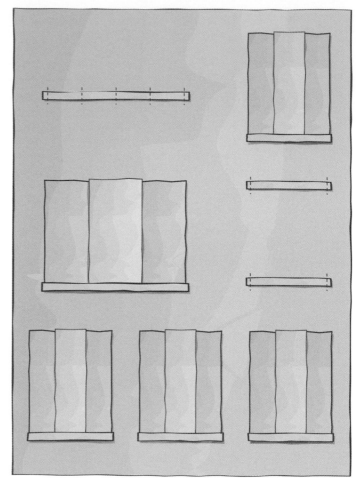

Step 12

Finishing

13 On the wrong side of the organizer back, adhere the double-sided adhesive to the batting. Peel the paper backing away and place the back and front wrong sides together. Iron the two pieces together and trim the edges if needed. Baste together around the edges.

14 Unfold the edge of your 1" wide bias tape that is slightly shorter than the other. Pin the raw edge of the bias tape to the edge of your back piece along one side. Begin sewing along the fold line of the bias tape.

15 When you reach the corners, sew to the very edge.

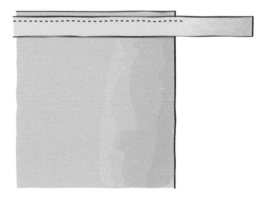

Step 15

16 Fold your bias tape back over your stitches at a 90-degree angle.

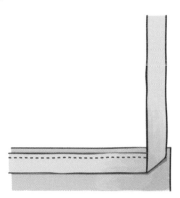

Step 16

17 Fold the bias tape back again, aligning the raw edge of the bias tape with the next side of your organizer.

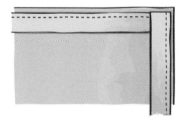

Step 17

18 Repeat Steps 15 to 17 for each corner.

19 When you reach your starting point, unfold each side of your bias tape completely and place the right sides together. Sew the ends together at a 45-degree angle. Finish sewing to the organizer.

20 Fold the bias tape to the right side of the organizer. Pin in place, creating tight miters at the corners. Edge-stitch along the fold.

21 With a grommet tool, place three grommets along the top of the organizer. To hang, install three hooks into the wall. (Try and place them into a wall stud if you can for extra stability.) Place the grommets over the hooks.

Herbal Sachet

Herbal Sachet

Sachets have a bit of an "old and dusty" vibe surrounding them. When I first considered doing a sachet, I immediately wrinkled my nose and thought, sachets? But I couldn't get the idea out of my head, so one day I decided to make one up. What resulted is one of my most favorite projects I've ever created. Whenever I open my drawer or closet, I am met with the sweet smell of lavender. Each time, I am reminded of the time spent making them with my children playing at my feet, and how my husband snuck over in the middle of the night to harvest the lavender from an obliging (public!) field.

Supplies

- **1 piece of fabric for the front, 8" × 8"**
- **1 piece of lightweight fusible interfacing for the front, 8" × 8"**
- **4 strips of contrasting border fabric for the top and bottom, each 7¼" × 1½"**
- **4 strips of contrasting border fabric for the sides, each 7" × 1½"**
- **2 pieces of linen for the back pieces, 6" × 5¾"**
- **2 pieces of lightweight fusible interfacing for the back pieces, 6" × 5¾"**
- **Miscellaneous wool felt scraps in coordinating colors**
- **Double-sided fusible adhesive**
- **6" strip of Velcro, ¾" wide**
- **Pillow stuffing (about 2 cups)**
- **Dried herbs of your choice (about 1 cup)**

Prep

1 Fuse the linen pieces for the front and backs with lightweight interfacing.

2 Fuse double-sided adhesive to the back of your wool felt pieces. Cut out the wool felt pieces using the patterns on page 161.

For the lavender sachet, you will need approximately 22 flower petals from four different shades of purple wool. Mix and match the sizes of the petals you use.

For the daisy sachet, you will need approximately 19 petals from two different shades of wool felt and the center piece.

Creating the Front

For the lavender sachet:

1 Iron the dark petal pieces onto the linen front approximately ½" apart in a tall oval shape. Continue to iron on all the petal pieces, randomly spacing the colors.

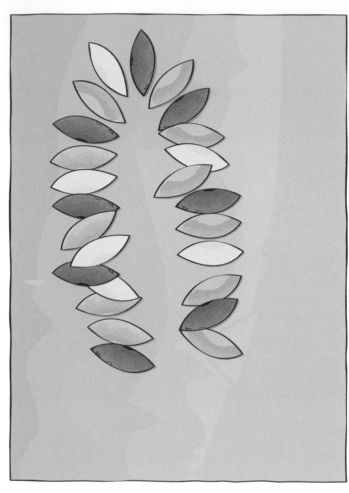

2 Stitch different colored French knots around the petal pieces. Make sure to sew at least one knot through each petal; this will secure the petal to the front piece. See the Introduction for a refresher on French knots.

3 Using a chain stitch, sew a stem through the center of the lavender. Make sure to have little stems going off into some of the buds.

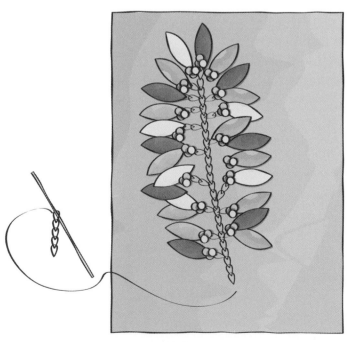

For the daisy sachet:

1 Iron on the center of the daisy onto the linen sachet front.

2 Iron on the individual daisy petals, alternating colors. Try to arrange the petals so the darker petals will be behind the lighter petals. Overlap the petals along the edge of the daisy center.

4 Embroider two rows of chain stitch down from the center of the daisy head for the stem.

Step 2

Step 4

3 Sew different colored French knots around the center of the daisy and the petal. Make sure to sew at least one knot through each petal; this will secure the petal to the front piece.

For each option:

1 Trim the front to 7½" wide by 6" tall.

Note: Because you handle the fabric so much during the French knot process, the edges can get a bit bent. Cutting the fabric to size after the hand sewing gives you a nice clean edge.

Adding Borders to the Front

1 Place one 7½" border strip, right sides together, at the top of the sachet front. Sew them together using a ½" seam allowance. Sew the second 7½" border strip to the bottom. Press the seams open in the back.

Step 2

Step 1

2 Sew the 7" border strips to the sides of the front the same way. Press the seams open in the back.

Forming the Back Piece

1 Take one piece of linen for the back and fold one 5¼" edge to the wrong side ½" and press. Fold 1" more and press again. Do the same with the other back piece.

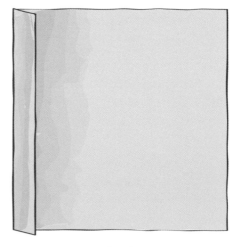

Step 1

2 Sew the male piece of Velcro onto the *right side* of the folded edge of one back piece. Sew along the two long sides of the Velcro.

3 Sew the female piece of Velcro onto the *wrong side* of the folded edge of the other back piece. Sew along the two long sides of the Velcro.

4 Stick the Velcro pieces together, lining up the top and bottom of the two back pieces. Stay-stitch at the top and bottom where the two pieces overlap.

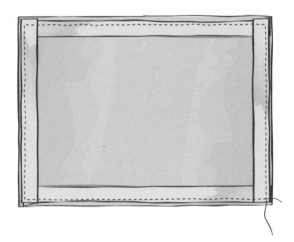

Step 7

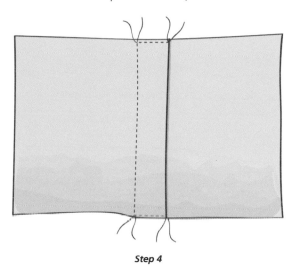

Step 4

5 Just as you did for the front, sew the remaining border pieces to the back. Sew one 7½" border piece at the top of the back piece and one at the bottom. Press the seams open in the back.

6 Sew the two 7" border strips to the sides of the back. Press the seams open in the back.

Finishing

7 Hold the front and back right sides together and sew all the way around the edges. Clip the corners. Turn right side out through the Velcro opening in the back. Push out all corners with a dull pointed tool (such as a pencil) and press.

8 Topstitch along the seams between the border and the front piece around the entire sachet.

Step 8

9 Fill your sachet with a combination of pillow stuffing and the dried herbs of your choice. (Experiment with herbs—I chose lavender for my lavender sachet and chamomile for my daisy sachet. Mint would be lovely also!)

Note: If your sachet starts to lose its scent, give it a good squeeze to release more of the essential oils from the buds. The Velcro closing on the back makes it easy to replace the insides when they truly lose their scent.

Garden Pillows

Garden Pillows

I find the outdoors especially inspiring and soothing, so I try to find ways to bring the outdoors in whenever I can. These leaf and chrysanthemum pillows do the trick. I used an earthy linen as the base and little pops of color in the leaves and petals.

Supplies

For each pillow:
- **1 piece of linen for the front, 20" square**
- **1 piece of lightweight fusible interfacing, 20" square**
- **2 pieces of linen for the back, each 16" × 20"**
- **Vellum or tracing paper**
- **2 pieces of lightweight fusible interfacing for the back, each 16" × 20"**
- **1 pillow form, 20" square**
- **¼ yard of double-sided iron-on adhesive**

For the chrysanthemum appliqué:
- **Approximately 40 fabric scraps from one color family (pink, purple, orange, etc.), each roughly 3" × 3"**

For the leaf appliqué:
- **Approximately 20 green fabric scraps, each roughly 2" × 3½"**

Prep

1 Adhere the lightweight interfacing to the wrong side of the linen for the front and the two back pieces.

2 Adhere the double sided-adhesive to the back of the scraps you will use for the leaf or the chrysanthemum. Cut out your appliqué pieces using the pattern pieces on page 161. Place a piece of vellum or tracing paper over the patterns in the book and lightly trace the shapes with a pencil. Remove the tracing paper from the book and darken the line with a marker. Cut approximately ten of each size for the leaf, or fifteen larger petals and fifteen smaller petals for the chrysanthemum.

Creating the Appliqué

3 Peel the paper backing off of the appliqué pieces and arrange in either the leaf form or the chrysanthemum form.

For the leaf: Start with larger pieces at the lower left corner of your pillow and arrange the leaves, gradually getting smaller in a diagonal pattern toward the center of the pillow front.

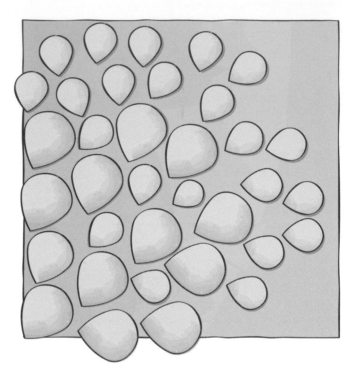

For the chrysanthemum: Start with your smaller petal pieces and arrange them in a half-circle starting about 5" from the top on the left edge of your pillow front and ending at the bottom edge of the pillow about 5" from the right edge. Working toward the lower left corner, layer the petals, gradually adding more of the larger petals. It's okay to overlap on the edges of the pillow front; you will trim it away later.

Press the pieces in place with your iron as you arrange them.

4 Sew the appliqué pieces. I used a small straight stitch on my machine with coordinating thread.

Forming the Pillow

5 Take one of your back pieces and press one of the long edges 1" to the wrong side. Turn 1" more, press, and edge-stitch along the fold line. Repeat with the opposite back piece.

Step 5

7 Place the back piece right sides to the front and pin together. Sew the pieces together around all four sides. Trim the edges.

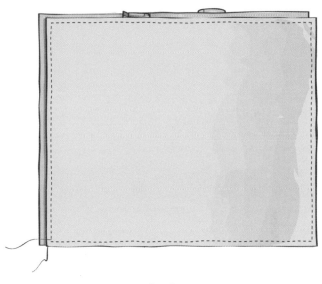

Step 7

6 With the back pieces right side up, lay the right side on top of the left, overlapping by approximately 8 inches so that your top and bottom sides each equal 20". Stay-stitch along the top and bottom edges.

8 Turn right side out through the opening in the back and fill with a 20" pillow form.

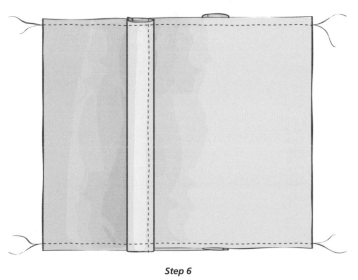

Step 6

Bubbly Shower Curtain

Bubbly Shower Curtain

Bubbles and shower curtains go together like rubber duckies and bathtubs. I actually tried to create something different for this project, but these sweet fish just wouldn't leave my mind, so I decided to run with it and came up with a fresh take on fish and bubbles in the bathroom! I found a shower curtain with a border that was similar to the fabrics I planned on using, but you could use any type. Try using a stripy curtain to mimic the look of seaweed.

Supplies

1 cotton or cotton blend shower curtain (do not use plastic)

Fabric scraps for the fish (this will make three fish on one shower curtain):
    3 fabric scraps for the fish bodies, each 4" × 8"
    3 fabric scraps for the small fish fins, each 2" × 2"
    3 fabric scraps for the belly fins, each 2" × 4"
    3 fabric scraps for the large tail fins, each 2" × 7"
    6 fabric scraps for the small tail fins, each 2" × 4"
    3 fabric scraps for the dorsal fins, each 2" × 3"

Fabric scraps for the bubbles:
    6 fabric scraps for the large bubbles, each 5½" × 5½"
    6 fabric scraps for the medium bubbles, each 4" × 4"
    12 fabric scraps for the small bubbles, each 2½" × 2½"

Double-sided adhesive for the backs of all appliqué pieces

Needle and embroidery floss

Prep

1 Apply double-sided adhesive to the backs of all fabrics you will be using for appliqué.

2 Cut out the shapes for the parts of the fish and the bubbles from the pattern pieces on pages 162–163.

Creating the Fish

3 Peel the paper backing off of the fish pattern pieces. Evenly space the three fish bodies on the shower curtain. Iron in place, then sew around the edges using a ⅛" allowance.

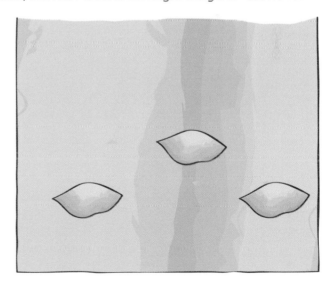

Step 3

4 Place the dorsal fin piece at the top of a fish and the two belly fins below. Iron in place, then sew around the edges using a ⅛" allowance. Repeat with the two remaining fish.

Step 4

5 Place the large tail fin coming off of the end of the fish body. Position two of the small tail fins on either side of the large tail fin. Iron in place, then sew around the edges using a ⅛" allowance. Repeat with the two remaining fish.

Step 5

Creating the Bubbles

6 Peel the paper backing off of the large bubbles. Space them across the shower curtain, about 12" to 18" above the fish. Iron in place, then sew around the edges using a ⅛" allowance.

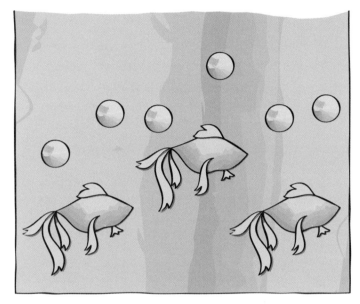

Step 6

7 Peel the paper backing off of the medium bubbles and space them across the shower curtain. Overlap with a few of the large bubbles. Iron in place, then sew around the edges using a ⅛" allowance.

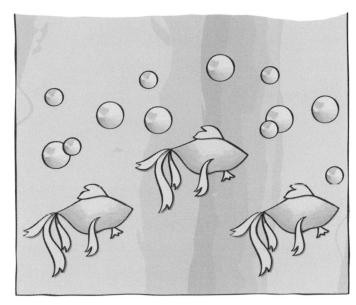

Step 7

8 Peel the paper backing off of the small bubbles and space them across the shower curtain. Overlap with some of the existing bubbles. Iron in place, then sew around the edges using a ⅛" allowance.

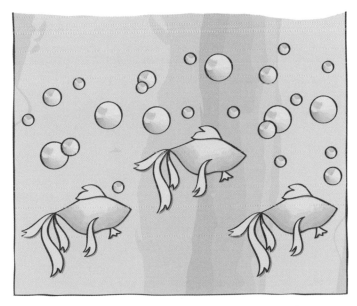

Step 8

Finishing

9 Using a needle and embroidery floss, sew some "transparent" bubbles with a running stitch around some of the fabric bubbles.

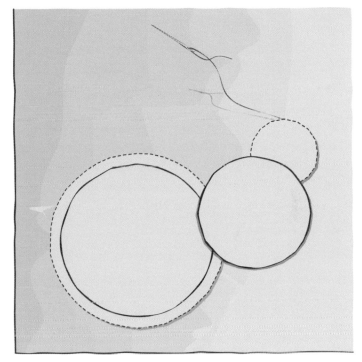

Step 9

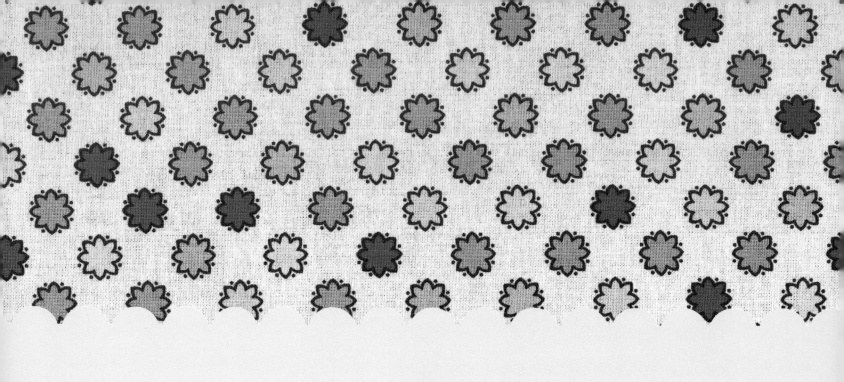

3

Children

Growing Tree Wall Hanging

Growing Tree Wall Hanging

I love the impact that this project makes when you walk into the room. And the fact that it records your child's height at different ages makes it a memorable keepsake. This would be a perfect baby gift for a dear friend or a special project to create for your own family. Instead of creating multiple trees, give each child their own color leaf and record everybody's heights on the same tree. I think ours will hang in our home forever, long after our children have outgrown the tallest branches.

Supplies

2 strips of brown fabric for the tree trunk, each 10" × 45"

1 piece of fusible batting for the tree trunk, 10" × 45"

1 piece of double-sided iron-on adhesive for the tree trunk, 10" × 45"

2 green rectangles for the treetop, each 24" × 15"

1 piece of fusible batting for the treetop, 24" × 15"

1 piece of double-sided iron-on adhesive for the treetop, 24" × 15"

50–80 brown strips of fabric, each 3" wide and in various lengths

80–100 green scraps of fabric for the leaves, each 4" × 5"

Note: My tree has 75 strips on the trunk and 70 leaves on the top.

Prep

1 Trace the large and small leaf pattern pieces on page 163.

2 From the green fabric scraps, cut out approximately 40 large leaves and 40–60 small leaves. Set aside.

Note: This project uses free motion quilting that is done with a special presser foot called either a darning or free motion foot.

Creating the Trunk

3 Fuse the batting to the wrong side of one of the tree trunk pieces.

4 Fuse the double-sided adhesive to the wrong side of the other tree trunk piece. Peel the paper backing off of the adhesive, place the two trunks wrong sides together, and iron.

5 Lay your tree trunk on your cutting surface. Starting at the bottom right-hand corner, cut a wavy pattern to the top of the trunk. Repeat on the opposite side. Cut out a few angled sections at the top for branches. Baste around all edges.

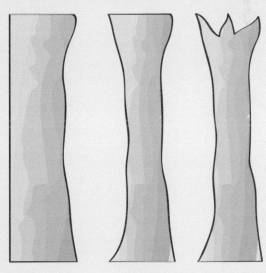

Step 5

6 Cut pieces of bark. Take the various 3" wide strips of brown fabric and cut wavy, irregular edges. Set aside your bark strips for now.

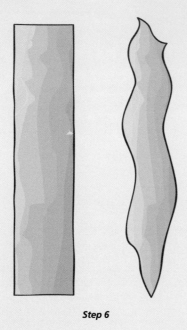

Step 6

Creating the Top

7 Fuse the batting to the wrong side of one of your treetop pieces.

8 Fuse the double-sided adhesive to the wrong side of the other treetop piece. Peel the paper backing off of the adhesive, place the two treetop pieces wrong sides together, and fuse.

Joining the Top and Bottom

9 Lay the tree trunk on top of the treetop. Baste together along the branches.

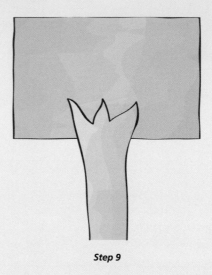

Step 9

Forming the Treetop

10 Lay the treetop on your cutting surface. Cut out the shape you want your treetop to be. Baste around the edges.

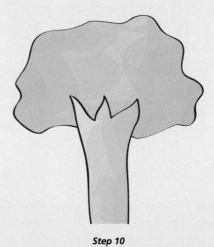

Step 10

Creating the Bark

11 Starting at the base of the tree trunk, pin several of your bark strips wrong side down onto the trunk. Sew in place with free motion quilting. If the bark pieces bunch up a bit here and there, that's okay. It makes the trunk look more realistic.

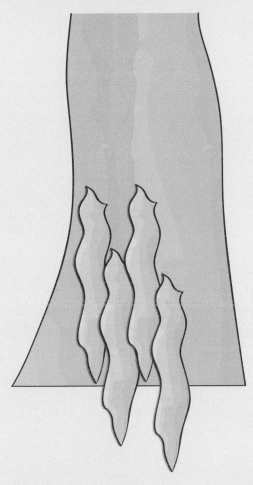

Step 11

12 Continue adding bark strips until you reach the top. Allow some bark to extend up into the treetop for realism.

Creating the Leaves

13 Place two fabric leaves wrong sides together and sew around the edges. Repeat with your remaining leaf pieces of the same sizes.

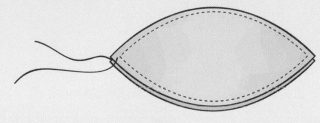

Step 13

14 Starting at the point where the branches enter the treetop, pin several leaves in place. Sew them to the treetop with a free motion stitch to resemble the veins of a leaf.

Step 14

15 Continue adding leaves until you are happy with the look of the tree. Set aside several leaves for use in documenting height in the future.

16 Attach to the wall with a series of small brads hidden between the leaves.

17 Every six months or so, measure your child's height. Write your child's age and height on the back of one of your surplus leaves. Measure the distance on the tree trunk and sew the leaf in place.

Colorful Brick Road Skirt

Colorful Brick Road Skirt

This delightful little girl's skirt is born out of very small pieces. I love taking tiny bits of fabric and making something as large as this. The color combinations are endless. Each tier could be a different color for a bright rainbow effect.

Supplies

40 fabric scraps (5 pieces each from 8 fabrics) for the skirt body (you will have a few spare pieces, depending on how you put your skirt together):

    Size 2: 2" × 5¼"
    Size 3: 2¼" × 5½"
    Size 4: 2½" × 5¾"
    Size 5: 2¾" × 6"
    Size 6: 3" × 6"
    Size 7: 3¼" × 6¼"
    Size 8: 3½" × 6½"

2 fabric scraps and 2 pieces of lightweight fusible interfacing for the waistband:

    Size 2: 4½"× 15"
    Sizes 3 and 4: 4¾" × 15½"
    Sizes 5 and 6: 5" × 16½"
    Sizes 7 and 8: 5¼" × 17"

14 strips of fabric for the ruffle (Note: If you do not have a serger, make each piece ½" wider than specified here; for example, 1¾" for size 2):

    Sizes 2 and 3: 1¼" × 40"
    Sizes 3 and 4: 1½" × 40"
    Sizes 5 and 6: 1¾" × 44"
    Sizes 7 and 8: 2" × 44"

1" wide elastic (measure your child's waist and subtract one inch)

Prep

1 Cut all fabric pieces out of prewashed and pressed fabric. Lay out your fabric pieces on your workspace in the order you will sew them together. You will need 8 rectangles for the top tier, 12 rectangles for the second tier, 16 rectangles for the third tier, and 20 rectangles for the fourth tier.

Forming the Patchwork Tiers

2 Begin with the top tier. Take two rectangles and hold them right sides together; stitch along one short end. Open the strip, hold another rectangle aligned with one short end, right sides together, and stitch together. Continue until all the pieces for the top tier have been stitched together. Stitch the first and last rectangles together to form a circle. Press and topstitch at each seam.

3 Repeat with the rectangles prepared for each of the tiers.

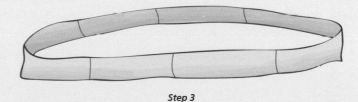

Step 3

Forming the Ruffles

4 Take the long strips you've prepared for the ruffles and sew them together into four circles as follows. Be sure to hold right sides together as you sew together the short ends of the strips.

- Use two strips to make a circle for the top ruffle.
- Use three strips to make a circle for the second ruffle.
- Use four strips to make a circle for the third ruffle.
- Use five strips to make a circle for the fourth ruffle.

Step 4

5 Hem each ruffle. I prefer to use a rolled hem on a serger, but if you don't have a serger, turn the hem a scant ¼" to the wrong side of the fabric and press. Turn under ¼" again, press, and stitch.

Note: Be sure to cut your ruffle strips larger to accommodate the extra turns.

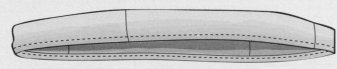

Step 5

6 Gather each ruffle to approximately half its size. I like to do this by sewing a loose running stitch ¼" from the unfinished edge of the ruffle and pulling one of the threads to gather it.

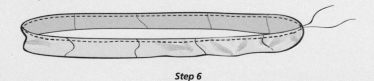

Step 6

Bringing the Skirt Together

7 Pin the unfinished edge of the top ruffle strip to the bottom edge of the top skirt tier with right sides together. Stitch in place using a ½" seam allowance. Repeat with the remaining tiers, using the second ruffle for the second tier of the skirt, and so on. Do not press the ruffle down yet.

Step 7

8 Loosely gather the top edge of each patchwork tier. With right sides facing, pin the top of the second tier to the bottom of the first tier, matching the raw edges and adjusting the gathers so that they are evenly spaced; the ruffle will be sandwiched between the layers. Stitch the tiers together. Repeat with the remaining tiers, matching the top of the third tier with the bottom of the second, and the top of the fourth tier with the bottom of the third. Serge or zigzag to finish the edges of the seam. Press the seams up and topstitch ¼" from the seam.

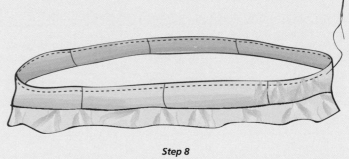

Step 8

Creating the Waistband

9 Fuse the lightweight interfacing to the wrong side of your waistband pieces.

10 Place your waistband pieces right sides together and stitch together at both short sides.

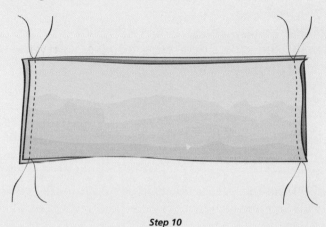

Step 10

11 With right sides together, pin the gathered edge of the top patchwork tier to the bottom edge of your waistband. Sew together, and serge or zigzag to finish the seam. Turn right side out, press, and topstitch along the waistband.

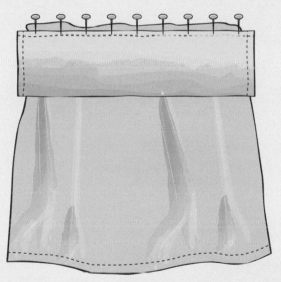

Step 11

12 Turn the top edge of the waistband over ¼" to the wrong side and press. Turn the edge over 1¼" to the wrong side and press. Sew around the bottom folded edge to create a casing for your elastic. Leave a 1½" opening unsewn to insert the elastic.

Step 12

13 Measure your child's waist and subtract one inch. Cut the elastic to this length. Attach a safety pin to one end of the elastic and thread the elastic through the opening in the waistband. Hold on to the opposite end of the elastic so it doesn't go through the opening. When you've fed the safety pin end of the elastic all the way through the casing, remove the safety pin and sew the ends of the elastic together.

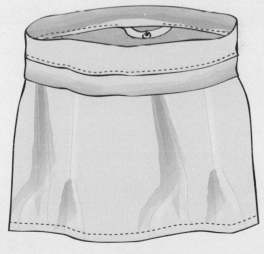

Step 13

14 Sew the casing shut. Press and enjoy!

Mary Jane Slippers

Mary Jane Slippers

What child doesn't need a sweet pair of slippers, just right for kicking around the house in? Make them out of cotton, corduroy, or wool felt; or make some up in a fancy satin or silk to go with a holiday outfit. An elastic strap makes them easy for children to put on themselves, and the ruffle and flower add a new touch on a classic design. Or, leave the ruffle and flower off and add a fun appliqué shape to the toe for the little boy in your life.

Supplies

- **2 pieces of fabric for the outer sole (see chart for sizing)**
- **2 pieces of fabric for the sole lining (see chart)**
- **2 pieces of fabric for the outer slipper body (see chart)**
- **2 pieces of fabric for the slipper body lining (see chart)**
- **Lightweight fusible interfacing for all shoe pieces. (see chart)**
- **Ruffle strip (see chart)**
- **¼" wide elastic for the strap (see chart)**
- **Fabric for the strap (see chart)**
- **2 pieces of wool felt, each 2" square, in coordinating colors for the flower**

Prep

1 Trace the slipper body and sole pattern pieces for your child's shoe size from pages 164–165.

2 Adhere the lightweight fusible interfacing to the back of the fabric you will be using for both the outside of the slipper and the lining.

3 Place the fold line of the pattern piece for the body of the shoe on the fold of the fabric and cut. Repeat for second outer body piece and the two lining pieces. Cut out two soles from the lining and two from the outer sole fabric.

Note: Depending on the size slipper you are making, you may want to sew them completely by hand. The pieces are somewhat small and can be difficult to maneuver around a sewing machine.

Shoe Size

	1	2	3	4	5	6	7	8	9	10	11	12	13
Sole	5" × 3"	5" × 3"	5" × 3"	6" × 4"	6" × 4"	6" × 4"	7" × 4"	7" × 4"	7" × 4"	8" × 5"	8" × 5"	9" × 5"	9" × 5"
Body	5" × 5"	5" × 5"	5" × 5"	6" × 5"	6" × 5"	7" × 5"	7" × 6"	7" × 6"	8" × 6"	8" × 6"	8" × 6"	9" × 7"	9" × 7"
Strap	2" × 4"	2" × 4"	2" × 4"	2" × 5"	2" × 5"	2" × 5"	2" × 5"	2" × 5"	2" × 6"	2" × 6"	2" × 6"	2" × 7"	2" × 7"
Elastic	2"	2"	2"	2¼"	2½"	2½"	2½"	2½"	2¾"	2¾"	3"	3"	3"
Ruffle strip	2" × 7"	2" × 8"	2" × 8"	2" × 8"	2" × 8"	2" × 9"	2" × 9"	2" × 10"	2" × 10"	2" × 11"	2" × 12"	2" × 12"	2" × 13"

Creating the Ruffle

4 Fold the ruffle strip in half with right sides together and sew together at the short ends to form a circle.

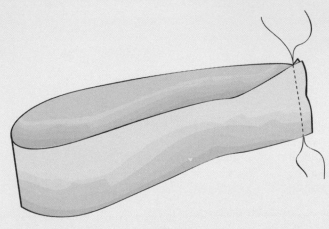

Step 4

5 Fold this circle in half lengthwise with wrong sides together and press.

6 Baste around the raw edge of the ruffle. Pull one thread to gather the ruffle to approximately half the original size.

Forming the Shoe

7 With the upper shoe folded on the fold line with right sides together, sew along the short straight edge at the bottom to form the heel. Press the seam open. Repeat with the lining piece.

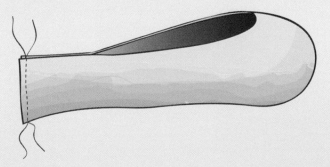

Step 7

8 With the raw edges together, pin the ruffle around the top opening of the outer shoe with the right sides facing out. Sew in place.

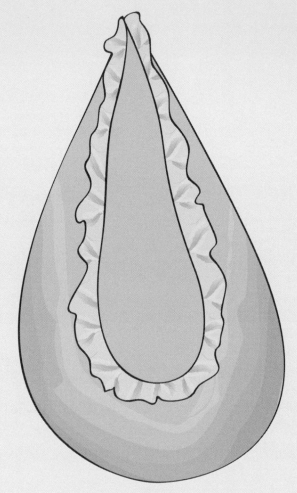

Step 8

9 Pin the top of the shoe to the sole with right sides together. Sew in place. Repeat with the lining pieces. Clip the seam allowances. Turn the outer shoe right side out, but leave the lining wrong side out.

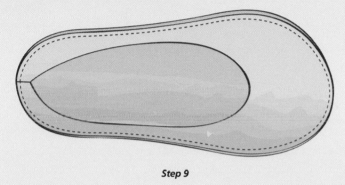

Step 9

Creating the Strap

10 Fold the fabric for the strap in half lengthwise with right sides together and sew along the long side. Use a turning tool such as the eraser end of a pencil to turn right side out.

11 Draw the elastic through the strap casing until the end of the elastic is at the edge of the casing. Sew in place.

12 Pull the elastic through the casing and sew it in place at the opposite end.

Step 12

13 Pin one end of the strap right sides to the outside section of the shoe, one-fourth of the way from the toe end of the opening. Wrap the elastic under the bottom of the shoe and pin in place on the opposite side. Sew the strap in place.

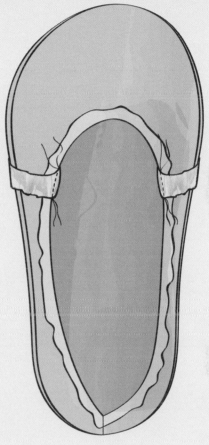

Step 13

Joining the Outside and Lining

14 Place the outer slipper inside the lining so the right sides are touching. Pin together and sew, leaving an open section at the heel that is approximately 2 " wide. Clip the seam allowances along the curves. Turn right side out.

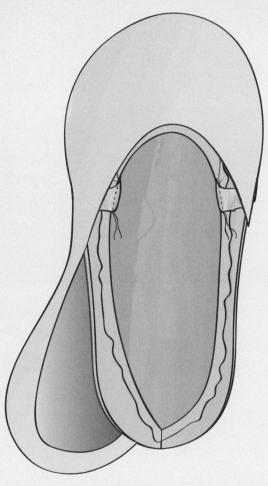

Step 14

15 Press the ruffle down and edge-stitch or blanket-stitch around the slipper.

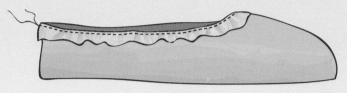

Step 15

Embellishment

16 Add a flower embellishment at the outer corner of the slipper by cutting your felt flowers and stitching them in place with a series of French knots. (Use the smaller flower pattern from the Cherry Blossom Tee on page 171.) See the Introduction for a refresher on French knots.

Step 16

Countdown Chain

Countdown Chain

Memories are born out of tradition. In our family, whenever we are looking forward to an event, we like to have a countdown chain. You probably made these out of construction paper in kindergarten. This is a slightly more durable version, one that will stand the test of time and store easily. It adds to the tradition of events in the same manner that using the same Christmas stocking each year brings back memories of times gone past. You can make as many links as you want—I suggest 31 so you will have enough for any month of the year.

Supplies

31 fabric scraps, each 4" × 12"

31 pieces of lightweight fusible interfacing, each 4" × 12"

31 squares of 1" wide hook & loop tape

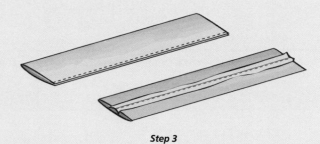

Step 3

Prep

1 Cut out your fabric pieces.

2 With your iron, fuse a piece of lightweight interfacing to the wrong side of each fabric link piece.

Forming the Links

3 Take one link, fold it in half lengthwise with right sides together, and sew the raw edges of the long side together. Press with the seam at the center on the inside of the link.

4 Stitch along one short end. Turn right side out and press.

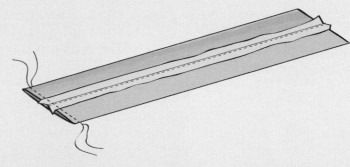

Step 4

5 Turn ½" of the raw edge of the remaining short end to the inside, pin in place, and press. With a ¼" seam allowance, stitch the opening shut, then continue edge-stitching around all sides of the link, ¼" in from the edge.

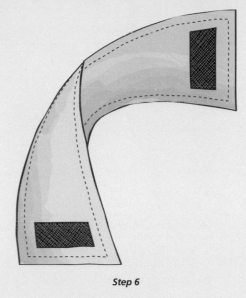

Step 6

Step 5

6 Separate the two halves of a hook & loop square and sew to opposite ends of your link. Make sure to place them so they will match up—one will be on the inside and one will be on the outside.

7 Repeat to create as many links as you need.

Note: You may find it quicker to make the links assembly-line fashion. Complete one step with all the links for your chain before moving on to the next step.

8 Thread the links together and hang them in a central spot in your home. When storing them, lay them flat on top of each other.

Woodland Bunny

Woodland Bunny

A whimsical companion for the Forest Owl (page 73), this delightful bunny is sure to please any boy or girl. I suggest making up both—every woodland creature needs a friend!

Supplies

2 fabric pieces for the body, each 10" × 15"

2 fabric pieces for the outer ear, each 5" × 10"

2 fabric pieces for the inner ear, each 5" × 10"

4 fabric pieces for the arms, each 3" × 7"

1 fabric piece for the belly, 5" × 7"

2 pieces of cream color wool felt for the eyes, each 1" × 1"

2 small black buttons for the eyes

4 pieces of fabric for the legs, each 2" × 13"

4 pieces of fabric for the arms, each 3" × 7"

1 piece of fabric for the base, 4" × 8"

2 pieces lightweight fusible interfacing for the body, each 10" × 15"

Vellum or tracing paper

Double-sided iron-on adhesive

Polyester fiberfill

Prep

1 Using vellum or tracing paper, copy all pattern pieces from pages 166–170. Trace the body pieces onto a folded piece of paper. Cut out all the pattern pieces. Unfold and layer the head piece over the top of the body and tape together to form the pattern for the full body.

Step 1

2 Iron the lightweight interfacing onto the body fabric. Cut out the body pieces.

3 Iron the lightweight interfacing onto the two outer ear pieces. Cut out all ear pieces.

4 Iron the double-sided adhesive onto the belly fabric. Cut out the belly.

5 Iron the double-sided adhesive onto the eye and nose fabric. Cut out the eye and nose pieces.

6 Cut out all remaining pattern pieces.

Creating the Face

7 Peel the paper backing off the double-sided adhesive on the eye circles. Place the circles near the center of the head, iron in place, and machine appliqué. Sew a small black button on each eye.

Note: If the Woodland Bunny is intended for a baby, you might want to embroider the eyes instead of using buttons.

Step 7

8 Peel the paper backing off the nose and place it wrong side down into the center of the face. Press in place. Sew the nose in place, and then embroider the mouth with a chain stitch, as shown.

Step 8

Forming the Body

9 Remove the paper backing from the belly piece. Place on top of the front body piece, aligning the straight bottom sections. Iron in place, then machine appliqué around the edges.

12 Pin the ear to the top of the head, pointing at an angle in toward the body. Sew to the head. Repeat with the opposite ear.

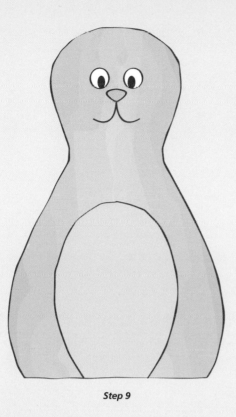

Step 9

Forming the Ears

10 Place one outer ear and one inner ear right sides together. Sew together, leaving the straight end open. Clip the curves, turn right side out, and press. Repeat with the pieces for the second ear.

11 Fold the ear in half lengthwise to the inside. Baste along the flat edge. Repeat with the second ear.

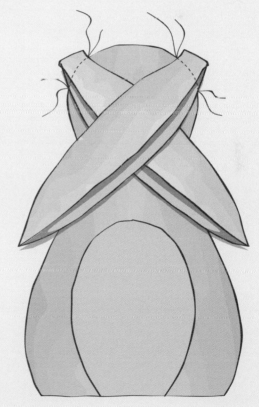

Step 12

Forming the Arms

13 Place two of the arm pieces right sides together. Sew together around the curved edges, leaving a 2" opening. Clip the curves and turn right side out. Gently stuff with polyester fiberfill and sew shut. Repeat with the pieces for the second arm.

Step 13

14 Pin the straight edge of each arm to the body, where the neck curves inward. Baste to the body.

Step 14

Forming the Legs

15 Place two of the leg pieces right sides together. Sew together around the long straight edges and the curved edge. Leave the short straight edge open. Clip the curved edge and turn right side out. Gently stuff with polyester fiberfill and sew shut. Repeat with the pieces for the second leg.

16 Pin the straight edge of each leg to the bottom edge of the front body piece where the belly section ends on each side. Baste to the body.

Step 16

Finishing

17 With the ears and arms tucked to the inside, place the back body piece right sides together to the front body piece. Sew together, leaving the bottom straight edge open.

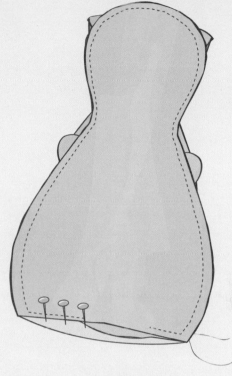

Step 18

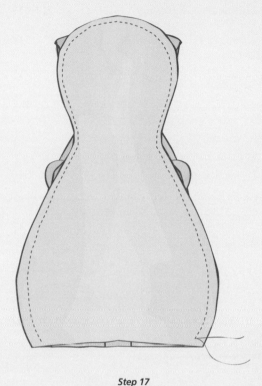

Step 17

18 Tuck the legs to the inside of the bunny. Pin the base right sides together to the opening at the bottom. Sew together, leaving a 3" opening. Clip the edges and turn right side out.

19 Stuff the bunny with polyester fiberfill. Use a blunt object, such as the eraser end of a pencil, to stuff the fiberfill into the body if needed. Use a needle and thread to close the opening with a whip stitch.

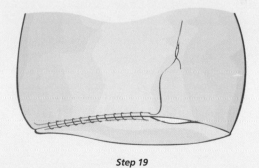

Step 19

Forest Owl

Forest Owl

Every now and then, you create something that you can't stop thinking about. Every time it floats across your mind, it brings a smile and maybe a chuckle. This wise owl is a great example. There is just something about this forest friend that I find so amusing. I think it is the general retro tone that I associate with owls: hip and cool, but cute and smart too. I designed this one for my kids, but he hasn't made it to either of their rooms yet. He sits perched on my desk, keeping me company as the day goes by.

Supplies

- 2 brown fabric pieces for the main body pieces, each 10" × 15"
- 2 lightweight fusible interfacing for the main body pieces, each 10" × 15"
- 1 fabric scrap for the belly, 5" × 9"
- 2 brown fabric scraps for the outer wing, each 5" × 9"
- 2 fabric scraps for the inner wing, each 5" × 9"
- 1 piece of double-sided iron-on adhesive for the belly, 5" × 9"
- 1 piece of double-sided iron-on adhesive for the eyes, 5" × 4½"
- 4 pieces of lightweight fusible interfacing for the wings, each 5" × 9"
- 2 squares of light-colored wool felt for the large eye circle, each 2½"
- 2 squares of medium-colored wool felt for the middle eye circle, each 2"
- 1 piece of wool felt for the beak, 1" × 1"
- 1 piece of double-sided iron-on adhesive for the beak, 1" × 1"
- 2 squares of dark-colored wool felt for the small eye circle, each 1"
- 2 pieces of wool felt for the ears, each 3" × 3"
- 1 piece fabric for the base, 4" × 8"
- About 20 pieces of coordinating colored wool felt pieces, each 1" × 1½"
- Vellum or tracing paper
- Polyester fiberfill
- Needle and embroidery thread

Prep

1 Using vellum or tracing paper, copy all pattern pieces from pages 166–170. Trace the body pieces onto a folded piece of paper. Cut out all the pattern pieces. Unfold and layer the head piece over the top of the body and tape together to form the pattern for the full body.

Step 1

Step 7

Forming the Face

7 Peel off the paper backing of the double-sided adhesive on the eye circles and beak. Place the large circles halfway down the head, iron in place, and machine appliqué. Layer the medium circles on top of the large circles, press in place, and machine appliqué. Place the small circles on top of the medium circles, press in place, and machine appliqué. Fuse the beak onto the center of the face and sew in place.

2 Iron the lightweight interfacing pieces onto the two largest fabric pieces for the body. Place the pattern piece onto the fabric and cut out two body pieces.

3 Iron the lightweight interfacing onto the four pieces of fabric for the inner and outer wings. Cut out the wings.

4 Iron the double-sided adhesive onto the fabric for the belly section. Cut out the belly.

5 Cut squares of double-sided adhesive the same sizes as the felt squares. Iron these onto all six wool scraps for the eyes and beak. Cut out the eye circles and beak pieces.

6 Cut out all remaining pattern pieces.

Forming the Body

8 Remove the paper backing from the belly piece. Place on top of the front body piece, aligning the straight bottom sections. Press in place and machine appliqué around the edges.

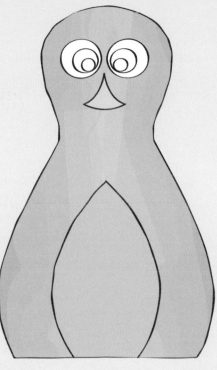

Step 8

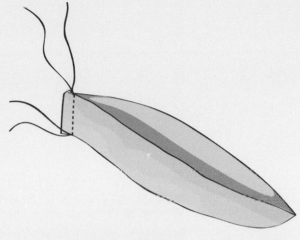

Step 10

11 Pin the wing at the shoulder joint, pointing at an angle toward the belly. Sew to the body. Repeat with the opposite wing.

Forming the Wings

9 Place one outer wing piece right sides together with an inner wing piece. Sew together, leaving the flat end open. Clip the curves, turn right side out, and press. Repeat with the second set of wing pieces.

10 Fold the wing in half to the inside. Baste along the flat edge. Repeat with the opposite wing.

Step 11

Forming the Ears

12 Fold one of the ears in half, with the pointed end at the top and the straight end on the bottom. Baste across the straight edge. Repeat with the opposite ear.

Step 12

13 Pin the straight edge of each ear to the top of the head above each eye, with the folded edge to the inside. Sew in place.

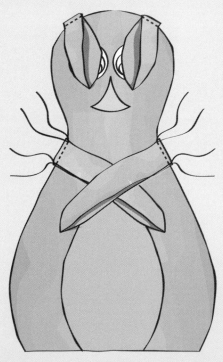

Step 13

Finishing

14 With the ears and wings tucked to the inside, place the back and front body sections right sides together. Sew together, leaving the bottom straight edge open.

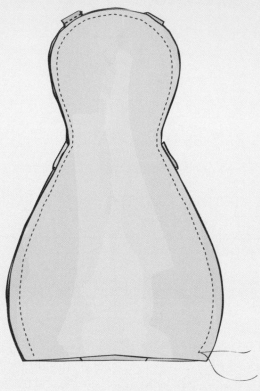

Step 14

15 Pin the base to the opening at the bottom of the owl with right sides together. Sew together, leaving a 3" opening. Clip the edges and turn right side out.

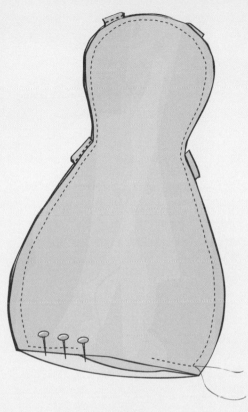

Step 15

17 Using a needle and embroidery thread, attach several wool felt feathers around the neckline and wings of your owl with French knots. If needed, add a couple of stitches at the top of the wings to help them stay down. See the Introduction for help on French knots.

Step 17

16 Stuff the owl with polyester fiberfill. Use a blunt object, such as the eraser end of a pencil, to stuff the fiberfill into the owl if needed. Use a needle and thread to close the opening with a whip stitch.

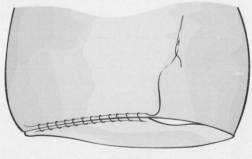

Step 16

Story Time Quilt

Story Time Quilt

Sweet and simple, this polka-dot quilt can have a big impact or a subtle one, depending on the fabrics you use. I've chosen conversational fabrics that have a fairy tale theme. My daughter keeps this quilt on her doll bed, next to the books. Whenever we have story time in her room, the quilt ends up on somebody's lap. There is something so cozy about snuggling up for a story with a quilt, and so was born the Story Time Quilt. I've chosen linen for my background, but a patterned background would be pretty, too.

Supplies

1 piece of pale-colored linen, 20" × 20"

1 darker piece of linen, 20" × 6"

1 piece of fabric for backing, 20" × 25"

12 pieces of fabric, each 4½" square (charm packs work well with this project)

1 piece of cardstock, about 4½" square

4 strips of fabric, each 44" × 5"

Needle and coordinating embroidery floss

Aluminum foil

Spray starch

Prep

1 Trace the larger circle pattern on page 171 onto paper and cut it out. Use this template to cut 12 circles out of your 4½" fabric squares.

2 Trace the smaller circle pattern on page 171 onto paper. Place it on top of the cardstock and cut out the circle.

Forming the Circles

3 Take a piece of aluminum foil about 6" square and lightly spray it with spray starch.

4 Lay one of your fabric circles right side down onto the spray starch.

5 Lay the cardstock circle in the center of the fabric.

6 Wrap the aluminum foil around the cardstock; this will wrap the fabric edges around the form.

7 Iron through the foil. Allow to cool, then remove the fabric from the aluminum foil and take out the cardstock. Press the fabric circle again. Repeat with the remaining fabric squares to create 12 circles.

8 Cut two of the circles in half using a rotary blade and mat.

Assembling the Quilt

9 Hold the two pieces of linen with one 20" side aligned, right sides together, and stitch together using a ½" seam allowance. Press the seam open.

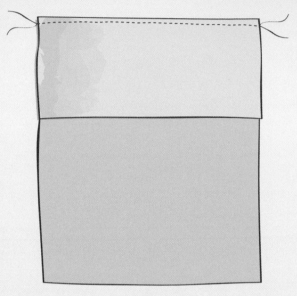

Step 9

10 Arrange the circles right side up on the linen. Pin in place. (You could also apply an adhesive to them, but they are small enough that I find pinning works just fine.) Arrange the four halves around the edges, and make sure to place at least one circle on the seam of the two linens. It adds a great contrast!

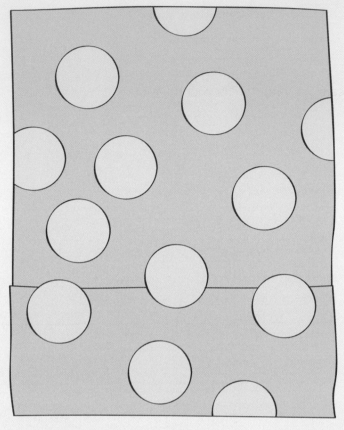

Step 10

11 Sew the circles onto the quilt. I used a straight stitch very close to the folded edge of the circles.

12 Working from the wrong side of the quilt, use sharp, pointy scissors to trim away the linen that is directly behind each of your circles. If there is any excess fabric from your polka dots, trim that away, too. Be careful not to cut into the stitching. This will keep the circles from being too bulky and to move with the rest of the quilt without being too stiff.

Creating the Ruffle

13 Hold two of the long strips with right sides together and stitch across one short end. Repeat with the other two strips. Sew these two long strips together the same way to create one long strip for your ruffle.

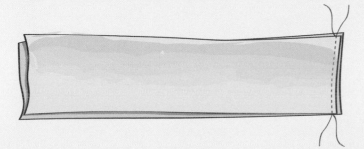

Step 13

14 Fold the ruffle in half lengthwise with wrong sides together and press.

Step 14

15 Adjust your machine to a long zigzag stitch. Starting 4" from the end of the ruffle strip, lay the embroidery floss down ½" from the raw edges of the strip. Slowly sew a zigzag stitch over the floss. Stop 4" from the opposite end. Pull the floss to gather the ruffle to approximately half its original size.

Step 15

16 Starting at the center of one long side, with the raw edges of the ruffle strip aligned with the edge of the quilt and the outside edges of the ruffle toward the center of the quilt, pin the ruffle around the edge of the quilt, adjusting the gathers so they are evenly spaced along the edges. Be sure to leave some "extra" gathers at the corners, so the ruffle will lay flat when it's done. When the ends of the ruffle strip meet, trim away the excess fabric from either end, leaving enough to overlap by 1". Open the fold in the ruffle and hold the two ends right sides together, then stitch the ends together. Adjust the gathers as necessary and finish pinning. Stitch the ruffle to the quilt, ½" from the raw edges.

Step 16

17 With the quilt right side up, place the fabric for the backing right side down on top of it. The ruffle will be sandwiched between the two pieces. Pin in place. Stitch together, with a ½" seam allowance, leaving a 6" section open on one side. Trim away excess fabric at the corners, being careful not to cut into the stitching.

18 Reach your hand into the opening and turn the quilt right side out. Fold the backing along the opening under ½". Press. Pin the opening shut and topstitch all the way around the edges of the quilt to close the hole.

19 Using a running stitch and embroidery floss, hand-quilt circles around your appliqué circles.

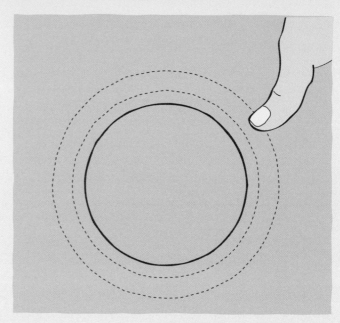

Step 19

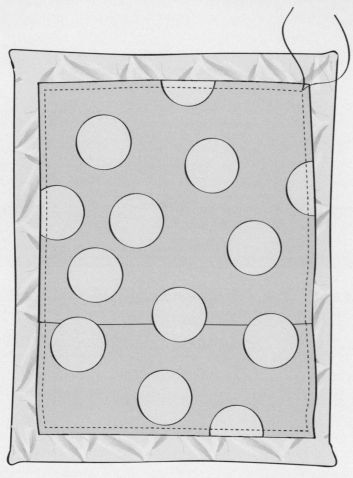

Step 17

Cherry Blossom Tee

Cherry Blossom Tee

This sweet tee is the perfect couch project. (I love those—they make you feel like you are still being productive during your down time!) Start with a store-bought tee, add some pretty flowers, and you have a shirt that will bring compliments from all who see it. Try using different textiles for this project. I used cottons and wool felt, but silks would also be lovely, or try felt for a baby. Washing in a machine will cause cottons to fray. Hand washing and a cool iron is recommended.

Supplies

1 store-bought cotton tee shirt, prewashed

Various coordinating fabric and wool felt scraps, each 2" × 2"

Various coordinating fabric and wool felt scraps, each 3" × 3"

Needle and embroidery floss

Prep

1 Trace the large and small flower pattern pieces on page 171. Use them to cut out blossoms from your fabric scraps. The number needed will depend on the size of the shirt and how many flowers you want. Cut at least six pieces of each size flower.

Sewing the Petals

2 Group the petals that you plan on sewing together. Try mixing a felt petal with a cotton petal. Experiment with different combinations of large and small petals, including some with small petals on top of large petals.

Step 2

3 Arrange the petals on the shirt as desired. I started with larger flowers at the shoulder and gradually trailed into smaller flowers. Pin in place.

Step 3

4 Sew each flower in place with a grouping of four to six French knots at the center of each flower. Refer to the Introduction for a refresher on French knots.

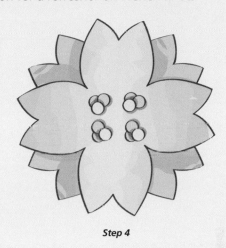

Step 4

Library Bag

Library Bag

Reading in our family is much more of a lifestyle-enhancer than a chunk of education. It's something we are passing on to our children, and weekly trips to the library are part of the process. Libraries are magical places. The smell, sights, and gentle sounds actually make me a little dizzy from joy. Our kids pick out two books each week and excitedly load them into their library bags. We store the books in the bags all week (as well as the library card) so there is never a lost book.

Supplies

1 fabric strip for the contrast strip on the front,
   5" × 15"

1 fabric strip for the left front, 4½" × 15"

2 pieces of fusible batting, each 16½" × 15"

1 piece of fabric for the back, 16½" × 15"

2 pieces of fabric for the lining, each 16½" × 16½"

2 pieces of fabric for the straps, each 4" × 18"

2 pieces of fusible interfacing for the straps, each
   4" × 18"

Prep

1 Cut out all pieces.

2 Fuse the interfacing onto the wrong side of the straps.

3 Fuse the batting to the wrong side of the bag back.

Creating the Front

4 Place your contrast strip right sides to the left front piece and sew together. Press the seam open.

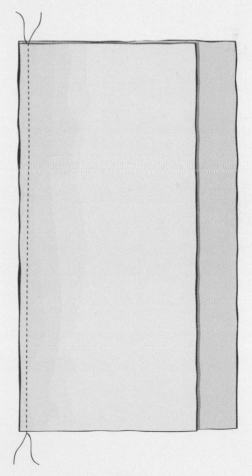

Step 4

5 Place your right front piece right sides together to the contrast strip and sew together. Press the seam open.

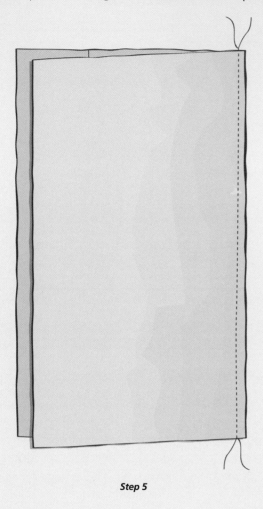

Step 5

6 Fuse the batting piece to the wrong side of the bag front.

7 Edge-stitch on each side of the seams at the contrast strip.

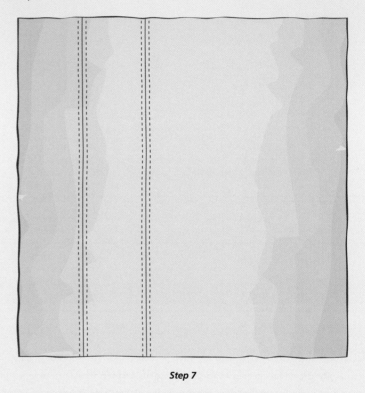

Step 7

Joining the Front and Back

8 Place your bag front right sides together to the bag back. Sew together along the sides and bottom.

Step 8

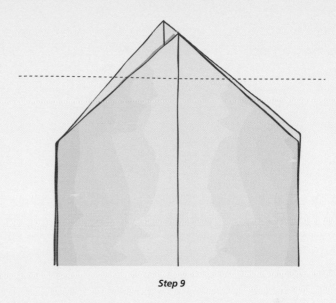

Step 9

Creating the Gussets

9 Fold the bag so the side seams are centered on the top and bottom, running down to a point. Measure 2" from the tip of each corner and cut off a straight line. Pin the opening you have made in place. Cut the other corner in the exact manner as you did this one and then sew each corner shut.

Forming the Lining

10 Place your lining pieces right sides together and sew together along the sides (15") and the bottom. (16½").

11 Create gussets in the same manner as you did for the outside of the bag.

Creating the Straps

12 Fold the straps lengthwise with wrong sides together and press. Open the fold. Repeat with the opposite strap.

Press the raw edges to the inside and press. Repeat with the opposite strap. Fold the strap in half again and press. Repeat with the opposite strap.

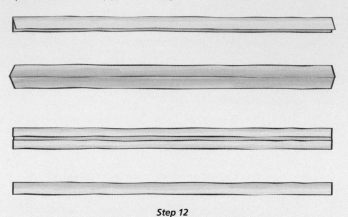

Step 12

13 Sew the strap along the folded edge and the open edge to close. Repeat with the opposite strap.

Step 13

Attaching the Straps

14 Pin one strap to the front of the bag, each end 4" from the sides. Sew in place. Repeat with the back side of the bag.

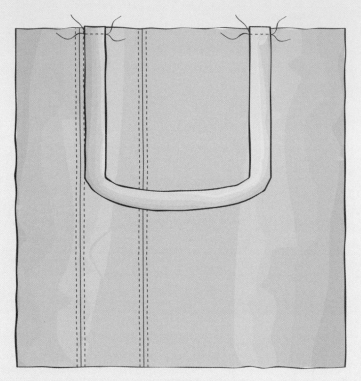

Step 14

15 Wrap each strap under the bottom of the bag and pin in place at the top edge of the back, 4" from each side seam. Sew in place.

Finishing

16 Insert the outside bag into the lining, with the right sides touching. Pin in place and sew together, leaving a 3" section open on the back.

17 Turn the bag right side out through the opening. Tuck the lining to the inside of the bag and press. Tuck the raw edges of your open section to the inside of the bag and press. Edge-stitch around the top of the bag to close the opening and finish.

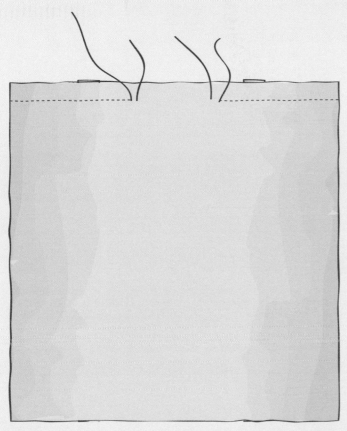

Step 16

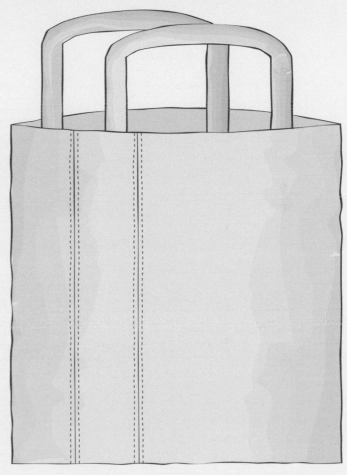

Step 17

4

Party

Party Lights

Party Lights

Nothing quite says "party" like festive lighting! String these lights in a tree for a special summer outdoor barbeque. Jazz up a birthday party, or string them along a child's headboard for an extra pop of color.

Supplies

Torn strips of fabric, each approximately 1" × 6"
Decoupage medium or spray adhesive
Disposable craft brush
1 strand white Chinese lantern lights

Note: These lights are easy to find during the spring and summer months in the outdoor section of general stores. You can also find them in some craft stores.

Prep

1 Remove the paper lanterns from the light strand.

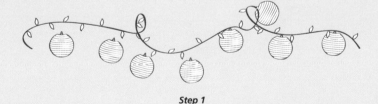
Step 1

Covering the Lanterns

2 With the craft brush, apply a thin coat of decoupage medium to a lantern. (Work on one lantern at a time so they don't dry out!) Alternatively, spray the lantern with spray adhesive.

3 Wrap each lantern with strips of colorful fabric. Tuck the fabric over the top and bottom edges of the lantern and secure with a bit of decoupage medium. Let dry for two to four hours.

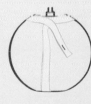
Step 3

4 If you wish, apply a coat of decoupage medium over the fabric to seal the edges and prevent fraying. Allow to dry overnight.

5 Re-attach the lanterns to the light strand, string it up, and enjoy!

Birthday Party Garland

Birthday Party Garland

This extra-special garland is sure to liven up any birthday celebration! It's not a quick project, but one I did over time—late-night movies with my husband, on a car trip with my mother and sisters . . . you get the idea! Like most things that take time, this garland is worth the wait. You could speed up the process by gathering the flowers on a sewing machine, but this is a labor of love. Each birthday is special, and I can't think of a better way to decorate (crepe paper, move aside!).

Supplies

Enough 4" wide fabric scraps to create a Patchwork Edge Trim, ½ inch × 12 feet (see page 124)

22 fabric strips, each about 2½" × 12", that are torn rather than cut along the long sides

42 fabric scraps, each 4" × 5" (the more varied, the better)

Vellum or tracing paper

20 buttons (I used fabric-covered buttons)

𝒩𝑜𝓉𝑒: The measurements given here will make a garland that's approximately 12 feet—long enough to drape wherever you like. You could certainly take out a few sections of flowers or flags to make your garland shorter.

Prep

1 Create a strip of ½" wide Patchwork Edge Trim about 12 feet long, or to your desired length. See page 124 for directions.

2 Using vellum or tracing paper, copy the triangle pattern from page 172. Using pinking shears, cut the 4" × 5" scraps into triangle-shaped pennants.

Forming the Flowers

3 Using a needle and thread with a knot on one end, sew a loose running stitch along one long side of a torn fabric strip. Pull the thread to gather the strip.

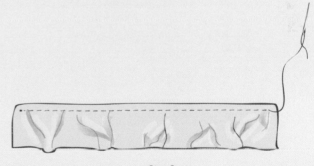

Step 3

4 Overlap the edges of the torn fabric strip and secure with a button in the center. Make a knot on the back of the flower and trim the threads.

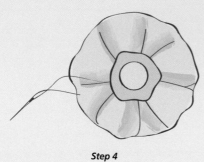

Step 4

5 Repeat Steps 3 and 4 for all flowers.

Forming the Pennants

6 Place two pennant sections wrong sides together and sew around the edges. Repeat with all pennant sections.

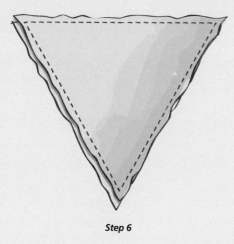

Step 6

Bringing the Garland Together

7 Beginning at one end, start sewing the Patchwork Edge Trim closed. After approximately 12", place the short end of one of your pennants inside the trim and sew it in place. Go another 2" along the trim, then add the next pennant. Continue spacing the pennants 2" apart until you've used them all. Leave a 12" tail of trim with no pennants at the end.

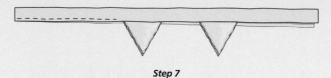

Step 7

8 Using needle and thread, sew a flower onto the Patchwork Edge Trim between each pair of pennants and at each end of the garland to finish the tails.

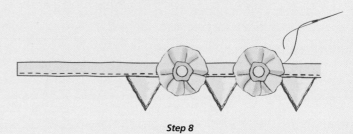

Step 8

Budding Treat Bags

Budding Treat Bags

These cute bags hold a wealth of options. I initially designed them to be used as party favors, but soon realized that you could do so much more with them! Our set sits on a wicker tray for easy transportation, with each bag holding a different art supply: crayons, pencils, scissors, glue, buttons . . .

Supplies

To make one treat bag, you will need:

- **2 pieces of fabric for the inside and outside of the bag, each 9" × 9"**
- **6 fabric scraps for the tops of the petals, each 4½" × 5"**
- **6 contrasting fabric scraps for the undersides of the petals, each 4½" × 5"**
- **Vellum or tracing paper**
- **Approximately 30" of single-fold bias tape in a coordinating color**
- **Approximately 15" of ¼" wide elastic**

Prep

1 Using vellum or tracing paper, copy the petal pattern piece on page 171 onto paper. Copy the large circle pattern piece on page 173 by folding your vellum or tracing paper in half, tracing the half-circle, and then cutting it out. Cut 2 circles from the 9" squares and cut 12 petals from the 4½" × 5" scraps.

Forming the Petals

2 Place two petal pieces with right sides together, one of the main color and one a contrasting color. Stitch together along the sides, leaving the long edge open. Repeat with the remaining petal sections to make six total petals. Clip the point, turn the petals right side out, and press.

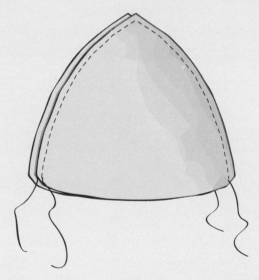

Step 2

Forming the Base

3 Place your circle pieces wrong sides together and stay-stitch around the edges.

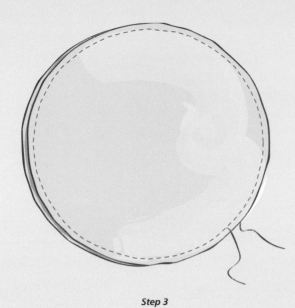

Step 3

4 Pin the petals around the edges of the circle with the points toward the center, as shown in the following illustration, and stitch in place. Trim away the excess fabric to ¼" from the seam. Press the petals out and the seams toward the circle.

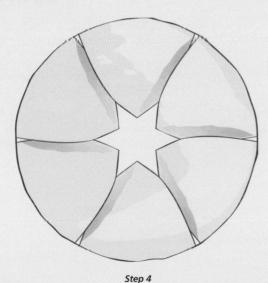

Step 4

5 Sew the bias tape around the edge of the base. Leave a ¼" gap between the ends of your bias tape. On each end, tuck the raw edge of the bias tape under itself to leave a finished edge.

Step 5

6 Using a safety pin to guide it, thread the elastic through one open end of the bias strip. Feed it all the way through the casing and out the other end. Sew the ends of the elastic together and tuck it back into the bias casing.

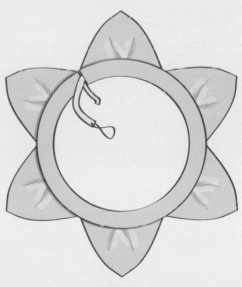

Step 6

7 Arrange the petals so they are pretty, then fill the bag with treats or whatever you like.

Caterpillar Invitations

Caterpillar Invitations

These came about from a desire to do something a little different for my son's birthday party invitations. I had store-bought cards that I loved, but I wanted to add a little pop and youthful flair to them. With a half-dozen scraps of fabric, caterpillars were born! You could use a similar layering technique to create ice cream cone invitations for a summer party or flower invitations for a girl. The possibilities are endless!

Supplies

To make each invitation, you will need:

1 patterned paper card, 4¼" × 5½"

(You can create this by cutting an 8½" × 11" piece of cardstock in half horizontally and then folding each piece in half vertically. You will get two cards from one sheet of cardstock.)

1 coordinating paper piece in a pale solid color, 3¾" × 5"

6 fabric scraps for the caterpillar body, each 1½" square

1 fabric scrap for the caterpillar head in a light color, 2" square

Spray adhesive or double-sided iron-on adhesive

Black marker for drawing the face

Glue stick

Embellishments such as buttons and ribbons (optional)

Prep

1 Trace the two circle patterns on page 171 onto paper. Use these patterns to cut out six smaller circles for the body from the fabric scraps. Cut one larger circle for the head from the 2" square of fabric.

Forming the Caterpillar

2 Place your first caterpillar body circle right side down onto scrap paper or an old sheet. Spray with adhesive and place near the lower left corner of the 3¾" × 5" paper. If you wish, sew around the circle (you can sew paper on the sewing machine). This isn't necessary because the adhesive will hold the fabric to the paper, but it adds a nice touch.

Step 2

3 Continue adding caterpillar circles in a wavy curve, ending the last small circle higher than the rest.

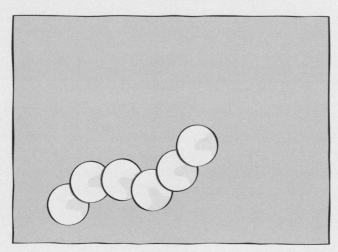

Step 3

4 Place the head at the top of the body circles.

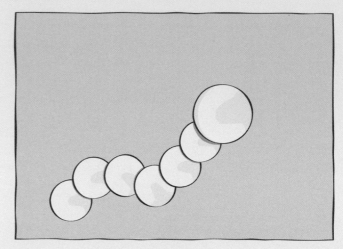

Step 4

5 Using a black marker, draw a simple face on your caterpillar: A half-circle smile and two oval eyes will do the trick. Add two antennae with dots on the end, and your face is done.

Step 5

Finishing the Card

6 Using a glue stick, adhere the wrong side of the caterpillar card to the center of the larger paper card. You should have ½" of border all the way around the solid caterpillar card section. You could sew these papers together if you wish.

Step 6

7 Add any extra embellishments to the outside of the card.

8 Add the date and time for the party to the inside of the card, and then get ready for the big day!

5

Crafts

Butterfly Pin

Butterfly Pin

My fashion sense seems to follow its own tune. I don't care for things that are too "in" and almost always prefer vintage over new. I like to mix textures and styles—something rustic with something feminine. And I always love to have a handmade piece worked into my wardrobe. These sweet butterflies definitely fit the bill for pretty as well as handmade. Whip some up to adorn your jacket or bag, or leave the pin back off and sew them onto pillows or attach them to a little girl's wall. Try them on Christmas stockings, pinned onto a birthday gift, attached to a hair clip . . . the possibilities are endless!

Supplies

Vellum or tracing paper

2 fabric scraps, at least 5" × 4" each

2 fabric scraps, at least 4" × 3" each, in a complementary color

Multipurpose spray adhesive

1 piece of canvas interfacing, 8" × 6"

Pin back

Wool felt piece approximately 2" × 2" in a color to complement the fabric you choose for the large wings

Needle and embroidery thread in a contrasting color

Craft glue

Buttons and trims (optional)

Prep

1 Using a piece of vellum or tracing paper, copy the patterns for the inner and outer butterfly wings from page 172 and set aside.

2 Lay one of the larger-sized fabric scraps right side down on scratch paper. Spray with adhesive. Lay the canvas interfacing on top and smooth it with your hand. Spray the canvas interfacing with adhesive and place the other larger-sized fabric scrap on top, with the right side facing up. Smooth it with your hand to remove any wrinkles, then press with a warm iron. Create a second sandwich the same way with the smaller-sized fabric scraps.

3 Pin the outer wings pattern on the larger "fabric sandwich." Pin the inner wings pattern to the smaller sandwich. Cut out both sets of wings.

Sewing the Body

4 Cut a 1" horizontal slit in the middle of the large outer butterfly wings.

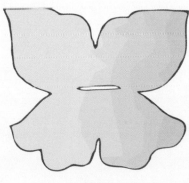

Step 4

5 Bring the lower edge of the slit up over the upper edge of the slit and stitch in place to create a pucker and add dimension to the wings.

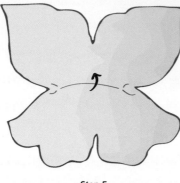

Step 5

6 Stitch around the edge of the outer wings. Try decorative blanket stitching or a simple running stitch. Repeat on the smaller wings.

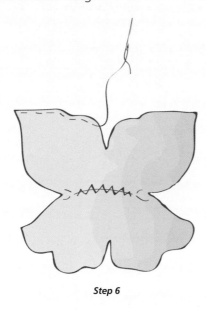

Step 6

7 Attach the small inner wings to the outer wings by making a few stitches at the center.

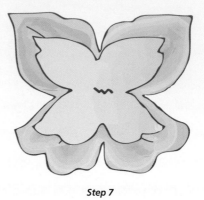

Step 7

Finishing

8 Sew a pin back to the center back of the outer wings.

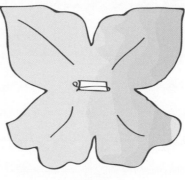

Step 8

9 Cut a felt circle large enough to cover the unsightly portions of the pin back. Make a slit in the center for the pin to fit through. Put a few drops of craft glue on the back of the felt and slide it into position, pressing it firmly in place. Allow to dry thoroughly.

10 Decorate the pins however you would like.

Fabric Gift Tags

Fabric Gift Tags

This is probably my favorite project for fabric scraps. These tags are quick and easy, and there is something extremely satisfying in joining paper to fabric by such an unorthodox method as melting plastic wrap between them! My kids love to help with this project—seeing the end result thrills them almost as much as it does me. I let them go to town embellishing the tags with the glue, ribbons, and buttons after I have ironed the pieces together and cut the shapes. This method also works with tissue paper in place of the fabric and can be used to make not only gift tags, but cards, calendars, ornaments, and custom scrapbooking paper.

Supplies

Vellum or tracing paper

Old towel

Cardstock in the same size as your fabric

Plastic wrap

Fabric scraps:
 For the oval tag: 4½" × 3½"
 For the round tag: 3½" × 3½"
 For the square edged tag: 2½" × 5"

Embellishment such as ribbons or buttons (optional)

Note: Double-sided iron-on adhesive also works well for this project.

Prep

1 Using vellum or tracing paper, copy the patterns you wish to use on page 172 and cut them out to create a template to trace around.

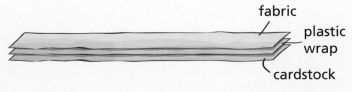

fabric

plastic wrap

cardstock

Step 1

2 Make a cardstock, plastic wrap, and fabric "sandwich." First, lay the old towel on your work surface (someplace safe to iron!). Place the cardstock on top of the towel (with the right side down, if there is a right side), lay a piece of plastic wrap on top, then place your fabric scrap, with the right side facing up, on top of that.

Note: Make sure to use an old towel, and avoid running your iron directly over the plastic wrap as it will be very hard to clean off. I know from experience!

3 Fold the towel over the sandwich. Apply the iron to your sandwich, making sure to keep the iron moving. Turn the whole thing over and iron again. The goal is to melt the plastic wrap to adhere to the cardstock and fabric but not scorch the paper. Let the sandwich cool before unwrapping.

Cutting

4 Lay the template of your choice on the cardstock and lightly trace the shape. Cut out your tag and use an eraser to clean up any pencil marks.

Finishing

5 Embellish the tags. Try putting a scrapbooking brad at the edge to string your ribbon through. Felt flowers and other trims will also look sweet, or you can create decorative stitching around the corners of your tags.

Yo-Yos

Yo-Yos

Yo-yos can be used anywhere you want to add a pop of color. Our family Christmas tree is adorned each year with a garland of red and white yo-yos. In olden times, entire quilt tops were constructed out of yo-yos, as well as toys with yo-yos for the legs and arms. This is truly a versatile little project, made even better by the fact that you can tote it anywhere!

Supplies

Vellum or tracing paper

Fabric scraps:
   For each small yo-yo, 5" × 5"
   For each medium yo-yo, 7" × 7"
   For each large yo-yo, 9" × 9"

Prep

1 Trace the pattern on page 173 for the size yo-yo you wish to make. For the large yo-yo, copy the large circle pattern piece by folding your vellum or tracing paper in half, tracing the half-circle, and then cutting it out.

2 Cut out the fabric for all the yo-yos you would like to make at one time.

Forming the Yo-Yo

3 Thread your needle with a length of thread and tie a knot at the end. You will use the thread double-stranded. About ¼" from the edge of the fabric on the wrong side, push your needle through the fabric.

Step 3

4 Folding the edge of the fabric to the wrong side about a ¼" as you go, sew around the circle, catching both layers of fabric, with long stitches (about ½").

Step 4

5 When you return to your starting point, pull the thread lightly to gather the yo-yo. You can either gather it tightly or loosely, it's up to you. Anchor your stitching on the back of the yo-yo and clip the threads. Arrange the yo-yo with your fingers and move on to the next one!

Step 5

Fabric-Covered Journal

Those traditional black-and-white composition books are the perfect size for journals. Close to a dozen of them float around our home. It is always a treat to find one and see what lies inside. Dinosaur sketches? The beginnings of penmanship? Incomprehensible scribbling? Whatever the inside holds, it always brings a smile to my face. These notebooks are inexpensive, at 50 cents to a dollar each. Glue on paper or fabric and a couple of scrapbooking embellishments, and you have a quick gift for under a buck. This version is a little bit fancier, complete with pockets to hold a pencil and a picture or two.

Supplies

1 standard sized composition book,
  7½" × 9¾"

2 fabric scraps for the small pocket sections,
  each 2½" × 4½"

2 fabric scraps for the large pocket sections,
  each 3½" × 4½"

1 fabric scrap for the pocket lining, 9" × 4½"

2 scraps of fabric (one for the outside cover,
  one for the lining), each 12¼" × 23½"

1 piece of lightweight fusible interfacing, 4" × 12"

Pens, pencils, or crayons tucked into the pockets
  along with a picture or two (optional)

Ribbon for gift giving

Forming the Pockets

1 Place the fabrics for the two small pocket sections right sides together and stitch together along one of the long sides. Press open.

Step 1

2 Match the long side of one of the large pocket pieces to one long side of the piece you made in Step 1, right sides together. Stitch together and press open. Sew the second large pocket piece to the opposite side so that the two small strips are in the middle and the two larger pieces are on the outsides. Press.

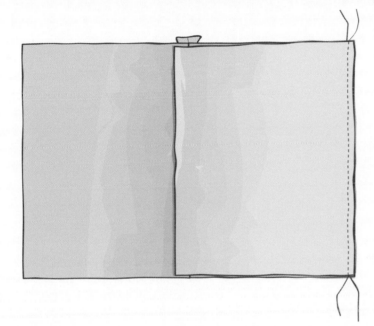

Step 2

3 With right sides together, pin the pocket lining to the pocket section you've just completed and sew the two together, leaving a 2½" gap at the center bottom. Clip the corners and edges.

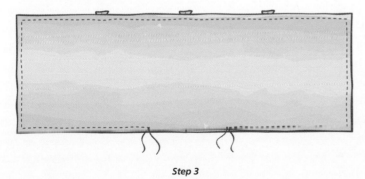

Step 3

4 Turn the pocket right side out through the opening. Tuck the raw edges of the opening to the inside of the pocket. Pin in place and press.

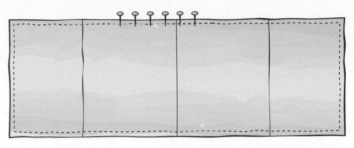

Step 4

Attaching the Pocket

5 Fuse the lightweight interfacing to the wrong side of the outside cover fabric.

6 Place the pocket, lining side down, onto the outside cover fabric. Center it 1½" from the bottom edge. There will be about 6½" on each side of the pocket. Stitch the pocket to the front cover along the sides and bottom of the pocket, stay-stitching at the beginning and end. Sew along the seams between the different pocket fabrics to create four pocket sections.

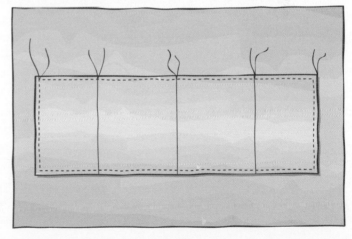

Step 6

Finishing the Cover

7 Hold the cover and cover lining right sides together. Leaving a 3" opening at the bottom center, stitch around all of the edges. Clip the corners.

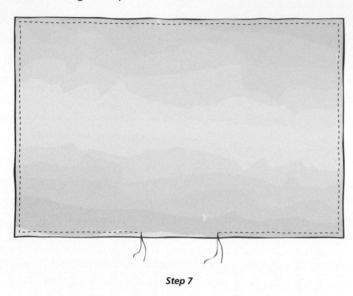

Step 7

8 Turn the cover right side out through the opening and tuck the raw edges to the inside of the cover. Pin in place and press.

9 Measure 3" in from each side and topstitch a straight line from top to bottom. Fold the cover to the inside, using this stitch line as your guide. Pin in place and press.

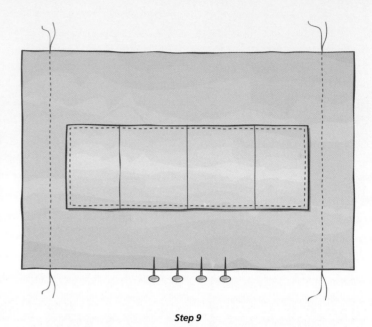

Step 9

10 Topstitch across the top and bottom edges. Make sure to close the opening at the bottom and to stitch the folded sides down. Press.

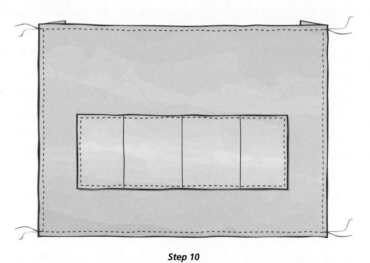

Step 10

11 Slide the composition book into the cover, wrap with a ribbon, and make someone happy!

Dahlia Pincushion

Dahlia Pincushion

I am of the mind that you can't have too many pincushions. I probably have one in every room of the house! I knew I wanted to include a pincushion in this book, and something with petals seemed right. I took inspiration from one of my favorite flowers. I love how the dahlia's petals curve out as they grow. Try a combination of colors—dahlias are known for being quite colorful. This pincushion goes together pretty fast, so you could easily put together several of them for gifts. If you chose holiday fabrics and felt colors, this could easily pass as a poinsettia.

Supplies

2 fabric scraps for the top and bottom, each 5" × 5"

1 fabric strip for the sides, 13½" × 2½"

2 pieces of lightweight fusible interfacing, each 5" × 5"

1 strip of lightweight fusible interfacing, 13½" × 2½"

6 wool felt pieces in a light color, each 2" × 2"

6 wool felt pieces in a darker coordinating color, each 2" × 2"

1 fabric scrap for the fabric-covered button, 2" × 2"

1 fabric-covered button kit, 1" size (available in the notions section of the fabric store)

Embroidery thread and needle

Polyester fiberfill

Prep

1 Fuse the interfacing to the top, bottom, and side pieces.

2 Using the pattern on page 173, cut out two small circles from the 5" square scraps.

3 Using the petal pattern on page 163, cut out 12 petals from the wool felt, 6 from the light color and 6 from the darker color.

4 Use the 2" × 2" fabric scrap and the button kit to create your fabric-covered button, following the manufacturer's instructions.

Forming the Dahlia Top

5 Take one of your wool felt petals and fold the bottom corners to meet each other at the bottom center of the petal. Using embroidery thread and a needle, stitch along the bottom edge of the petal as shown. Repeat with the remaining petals.

Step 5

6 With your needle and thread, attach the six darker petals to the top circle piece, leaving a 1" opening in the center of the flower.

Step 6

7 Sew the lighter-colored petals, alternating between the dark petals, ½" closer to the center.

Step 7

Putting the Pincushion Together

8 Fold the 13½" × 2½" fabric strip for the sides in half, right sides together, so that the two short ends meet. Stitch along the short end, using a ½" seam allowance to create a circle to form the sides of the pincushion.

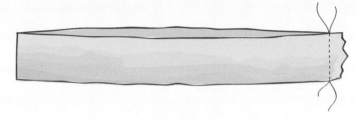

Step 8

9 Pin the right sides of the side strip to the edge of the dahlia top, taking care not to catch any of the petals in the seam. Stitch together. Cut notches around the seam.

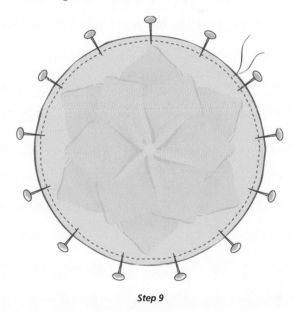

Step 9

10 With the right sides together, pin the bottom circle to the open edge of the side strip and sew these together, leaving a 2" opening. Cut notches around the seam. Turn right side out.

Finishing

11 Stuff tightly with polyester fiberfill.

12 Using a whip stitch, close the opening at the bottom of the pincushion.

13 Poke a long threaded needle through the center top of the pincushion. Push it through the bottom, take a small stitch, and push it back up through the top. Tighten the pincushion a bit, then use the needle and embroidery thread to attach the fabric-covered button. Tighten and knot the thread under the button.

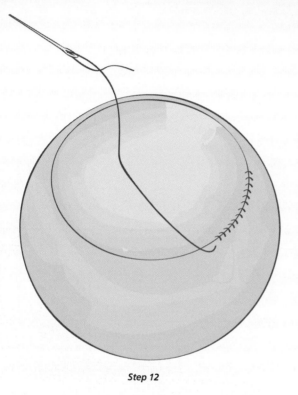

Step 12

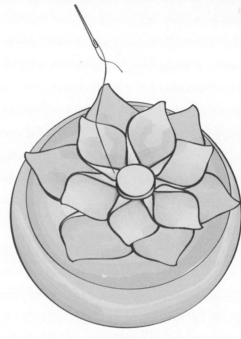

Step 13

Patchwork Edge Trim

Patchwork Edge Trim

Bright and colorful, this trim is a true scrap buster! You need only small pieces of fabric to trim a large project. This trim is similar to bias tape, but it is not cut on the bias, so I wouldn't suggest using it for projects that need the bend that bias tape provides. This trim is used in the Birthday Party Garland on page 97 and the Fruit Appliqué Tablecloth on page 9.

Supplies

For ½" wide trim: various lengths of 2" wide fabric scraps, cut with straight edges

For 1" wide trim: various lengths of 4" wide fabric scraps, cut with straight edges

For 2" wide trim: various lengths of 8" wide fabric scraps, cut with straight edges

Prep

1 Cut all pieces of fabric, making sure all of the edges are straight.

Forming the Trim

2 With right sides together, sew the strips of fabric together to form a long strip 2" (4", 8") wide.

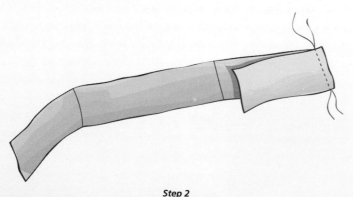

Step 2

3 Fold the strip in half lengthwise with wrong sides facing. Press.

Step 3

4 Open the strip and fold the raw edges to the inside using the fold line in the center as your guide. Press.

Step 4

5 Fold in half again so the raw edges are inside the trim. Press.

Step 5

6 Follow directions in the individual projects for ways to use this fun edging, or think up some ways of your own!

Picnic Quilt

Picnic Quilt

This simple quilt has quickly become my favorite, and I find myself searching out new fabric combinations with which to make it. It is laid-back quilting at its best. Every single piece is the same shape, so it's a perfect project for a Sunday afternoon when you want to be in the same room as your family, but keep your hands busy at the same time. I sewed this quilt on a machine, but someday I will make one entirely by hand. The finished quilt is approximately 63" wide by 76" long.

Supplies

Tracing paper

Cardstock

Aluminum foil

Spray starch

Rotary blade and mat

80 coordinating fabric scraps, each at least 12" × 11"

1 yard of fabric for making binding, 45" wide

Approximately 3 yards of fabric for the borders, 45" wide

Approximately 2½ yards each of two different fabrics for the backing, 45" wide

Batting of choice

Prep

1 Fold a piece of tracing paper in half. Open it up, place the fold line on the straight edge of the half-scallop shape on page 174, and trace the larger scallop onto the paper. Do the same with a second piece of paper and the smaller half-scallop. With the paper folded again, cut out both shapes to create two scallops. Use the smaller pattern piece to cut one scallop out of cardstock.

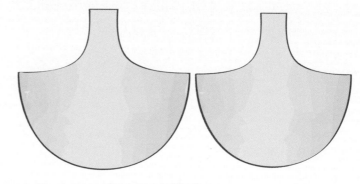

Step 1

Forming the Scallops

2 Using the larger scallop pattern piece, cut out 80 scallops from your fabric scraps.

3 Turn the bottom rounded edge of each scallop to the wrong side of the fabric ½". The easiest way to do this is to use the cardstock form as your guide. Lay down a piece of aluminum foil and lightly spray it with spray starch. Lay your fabric scallop right side down onto the foil. Align the top of the cardstock scallop with the top of the fabric scallop. Wrap the foil around the bottom edge of the cardstock. This will turn the fabric for you. Iron through the aluminum foil. This will give you perfectly rounded edges.

(I found this method on the blog of one of my fabric designer friends, Anna Maria Horner. Thank you for the amazing tip, Anna!)

4 Repeat this method for all the scallops. You will have a nice smooth curve on the front with the gathers from the turned edge on the wrong side.

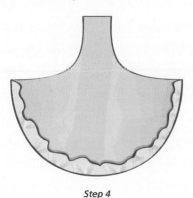

Step 4

Piecing the Quilt

5 With a rotary blade and mat, cut eight of scallops in half vertically.

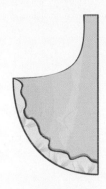
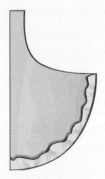

Step 5

6 Take one of the half-scallops that has the cut edge on the left. Place it on your rotary mat or another work surface with straight edges to keep things lined up. Place a full scallop to the right of the half scallop so they just touch.

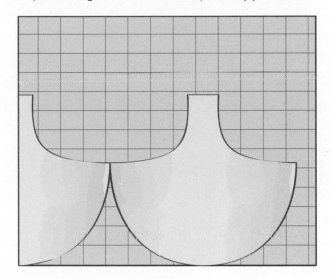

Step 6

7 Place a full scallop on top of these two pieces, so that the widest point of this scallop lines up with the tops of the first two pieces. This piece will overlap the lower two by about an inch. Pin in place and stitch along the curved edge where the pieces overlap.

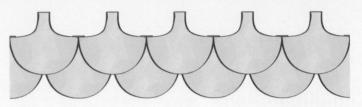

Step 9

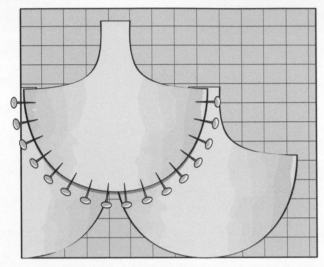

Step 7

10 Once you have the first two rows established, you can pin on an entire row at once and attach the scallops with one continuous seam. Every other row will start and end with half-scallops. Continue adding scallops until you have 16 rows.

8 Place another full scallop to the right on the bottom layer. Pin the next scallop in the valley you just created and stitch in place.

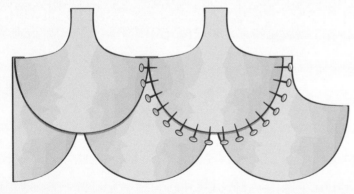

Step 8

9 Continue adding scallops in this manner until you have four scallops across the bottom layer plus half-scallops on each side and five full scallops on the second layer.

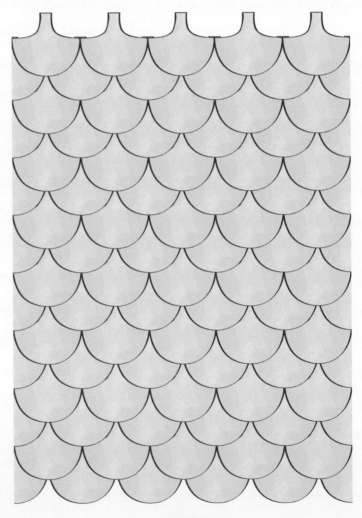

Step 10

11 Press the quilt top and trim the top and bottom edges so they are straight. Also trim excess fabric on the wrong side of the quilt. You don't want more than ¼" of fabric on your seams.

Step 11

Note: If you are using a directional fabric, be sure to cut your side borders along the length and not the width.

Adding the Borders

12 Measure your finished length and cut two 10" wide strips of border fabric to the length of your quilt. With right sides together, sew them to each long side of your quilt. Open the borders and press open your seams on the wrong side of the quilt. These will be your side borders.

Step 12

13 From a folded 45" width of fabric, cut four 10" sections. These will be your top and bottom borders.

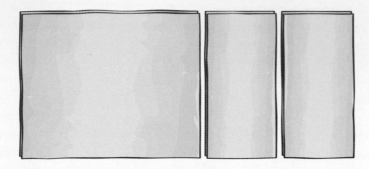

Step 13

14 Place two of the strips right sides together and sew together along the short edge to form the top border strip. Turn right side out and press the seam open on the inside. Repeat with the other two 10" pieces to form the bottom border strip.

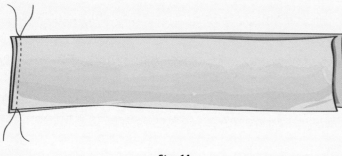

Step 14

15 Place the top border strip right sides to the quilt top edge. Align your border seam in the center of the quilt and sew the border to the quilt top. Using a rotary blade or scissors, cut away the excess border on each side of the quilt. Open your borders so the right sides are facing out and press the inside seams open. Repeat with the bottom border strip.

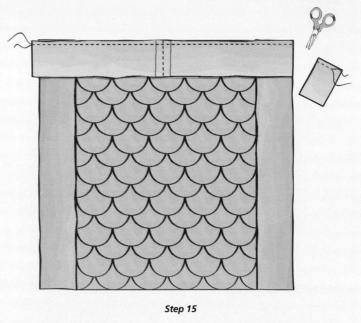

Step 15

Finishing the Quilt

16 Prepare the backing. Measure your final quilt length. Cut two lengths of folded 45" fabric to 8" longer than the length of your quilt. (This will really depend on how you plan on quilting it. If you are hand-quilting, you shouldn't need to cut the backing longer, but most professional quilters require the backing of the quilt to be larger than the quilt top.)

17 Remove the selvedges from the backing fabrics and place right sides together. Sew together along one long edge. Open the backing and press the inside seam open.

18 Make a quilt "sandwich" with the backing right side down, the batting in the middle, and the quilt top facing right side up. Your backing will be wide enough that you can offset the seam if you want, giving the back an interesting break-up of patterns.

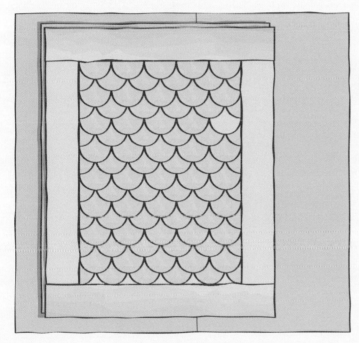

Step 18

19 Have the quilt quilted, either by a long arm quilter or by hand.

Binding the Quilt

20 Open the yard of fabric you have chosen for the binding so the wrong side is facing you with the fold in the center. Pull one corner diagonally toward the opposite corner.

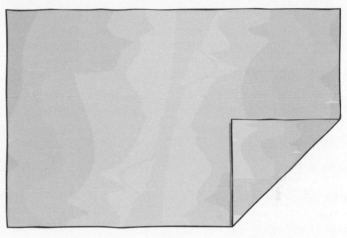

Step 20

21 You will have a triangle now. Turn your triangle 45 degrees so the fabric is on the bias and, with a rotary blade, cut enough 2½" strips of fabric to border your quilt.

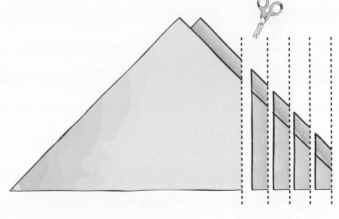

Step 21

22 Open your strips so they are right side up. The grain will now run diagonally. This is the entire purpose of cutting your strips on the bias; it will allow the fabric to curve with your project. Place two of your strips right sides together, forming a 90-degree angle. Sew the strips together at a 45-degree angle. Trim away the excess to a ¼" seam allowance and press the seams open. Repeat with the remaining strips to form one long border strip.

23 Fold the strip in half lengthwise with wrong sides together lengthwise and press. Open the strip so the wrong side is facing you. Fold the raw edges in toward the center fold and press. Fold the strip on the original crease so the raw edges are enclosed on the inside and press again.

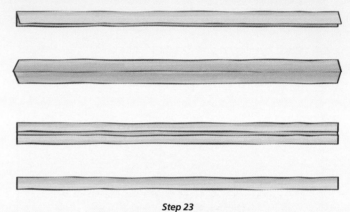

Step 23

24 Unfold one edge of your bias tape. Pin the raw edge of the tape against the raw edge of your quilt top all the way around, leaving 4–5" of overlap where the two ends meet.

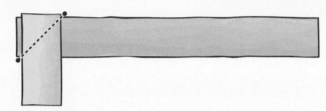

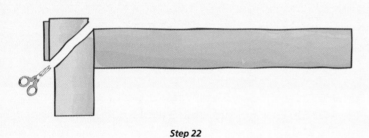

Step 22

25 Sew the bias tape to the quilt top, using the first fold line on the bias as your sewing guide. When you reach the corners, sew to the very edge.

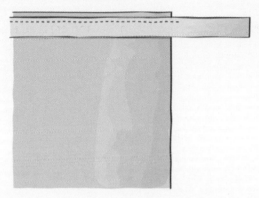

Step 25

26 Fold your bias tape back over your stitches at a 90-degree angle as shown.

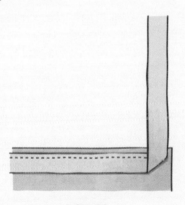

Step 26

27 Fold the bias tape back again, aligning the raw edge of the tape with the next side of your quilt. Repeat for each corner.

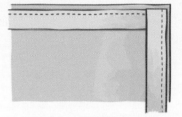

Step 27

28 When you reach your starting point, unfold each end of your bias tape completely and overlap with right sides together. Sew the ends together at a 45-degree angle. Finish sewing the binding to the quilt.

29 Fold the bias tape to the wrong side of the quilt. Pin in place, creating tight miters at the corners. Whip stitch along the folded edge of the bias to secure to the quilt backing.

Scrappy Silhouettes

Scrappy Silhouettes

First popular in the early nineteenth century as an inexpensive alternative to photography, silhouettes have become a timeless craft. In today's age of digital-this and easy-print that, silhouettes are regarded more as artistic projects. Traditionally, a silhouette is created by holding a light source in front of your subject with a piece of paper behind him or her on which to trace the shadow. But with the advent of digital cameras and a plethora of personal printers and print shops, you can create a silhouette easily—and without tears from a child who doesn't want to sit still for 45 minutes to have his or her shadow traced!

Supplies

1 picture frame
Paint for your frame (optional)
Background fabric slightly larger than your frame
¼" fusible batting slightly larger than your frame
Patterned fabric large enough for your silhouette image
Double-sided iron-on adhesive
Needle and embroidery thread (optional)
Hot glue gun

Prep

1 Take your frame apart and paint it if desired. Set aside and allow it to dry.

2 Measure the backing of your frame and cut your batting and background fabric 1½" larger on all sides. Fuse the batting to the wrong side of the background fabric.

Creating the Silhouette

3 Take a photograph of your subject. The best silhouette images of people are in profile, but don't be afraid to try straight-on angles for flowers, animals, and other subjects. Enlarge your photo so that the silhouette image is the right size for your frame. Carefully cut out the silhouette image.

Note: Enlarging a photograph is quite easy. You can do it on virtually any photo-editing program and print it out on your home printer, or take your photo to a print shop and enlarge it there.

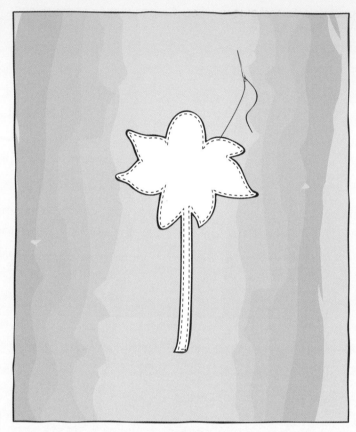

5 Peel the paper backing off of the double-sided adhesive and arrange it in place on the background fabric. Press in place. Appliqué in place either by machine or by hand using a needle and embroidery thread.

Step 3

4 Adhere the double-sided adhesive to the wrong side of the fabric you are using for the silhouette image. Using the image you cut from the photograph, carefully trace the silhouette onto the right side of the fabric. If you would like the image to be in reverse, trace it onto the wrong side of the fabric. Carefully cut out the silhouette image inside the tracing line.

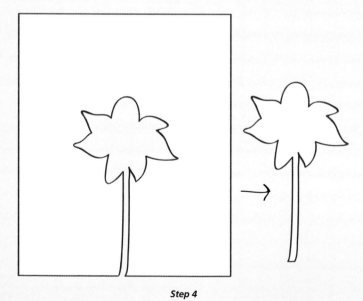

Step 4

Step 5

Finishing

6 Stretch the background fabric around the frame backing. Use a hot glue gun to adhere it on the wrong side of the backing along one side. Stretch the fabric to the opposite side and glue in place. Glue the fabric to the top and bottom, being careful to keep the fabric smooth and even in the front.

Step 6

7 Insert the picture into the frame. If the frame is old and has lost the tabs that hold the picture in place, secure it in place with glue.

6

Adults

Saturday Market Skirt

Saturday Market Skirt

For my family, Saturdays are both relaxing and busy. We usually end up at our local farmers market. The night before, I plan our menu for the week and make note of the fresh veggies, fruits, and other goodies I want to buy the next day. Honey for toast? Sure. Fresh flowers for the table? Almost always! After the farmers market, we usually hop over to what our town calls "Saturday Market," where local artisans display their goods. You can find everything: paintings, photography, clothing, and accessories galore. It's an earthy mix of our local talent. This skirt fits in so well with that environment. It's eclectic and a bit funky. Add a breezy top, and you'll have an outfit perfect for a day of market-hopping, topped with lunch in the park.

Supplies

Fabric scraps (see charts at right to find the requirements for your size)
Fabric for waistband and drawstring
Lightweight fusible interfacing

Prep

1 Cut your squares and waistband pieces according to the chart.

Note: In these instructions each square is cut to the same size, but try cutting a piece of each fabric you use over the next few months and not planning the skirt at all. When you have enough squares, make up the skirt—it will tell the story of your sewing!

Women's sizes: Cut 56 squares to the dimensions below. Cut 2 waistband pieces to the measurements below.

	XS	S	M	L	XL	XXL	XXXL
Square size	7½"	7¾"	8"	8¼"	8½"	9"	9½"
Waistband height	6½"	6½"	6¾"	7"	7¼"	7½"	7¾"
Waistband length	17½"	19"	20"	21"	22½"	24"	25½"

Children's sizes: Cut 36 squares for sizes 12/18m, 2y, and 3/4y; cut 56 squares for sizes 5/6 and 7/8 to the dimensions below. Cut 2 waistband pieces to the measurements below.

	12m/18m	2y	3/4y	5/6y	7/8y
Square size	5"	5½"	5¾"	6"	6¼"
Waistband height	4¼"	4½"	4¾"	5"	5¼"
Waistband length	14½"	15"	15½"	16½"	17"

Sewing the Skirt

2 Using a ¼" seam allowance, sew eight squares into a strip. Press and topstitch each seam.

Step 2

3 Fold the strip in half, with right sides together, and sew the end squares together to form a circle. Press the seam and topstitch. This is your first tier.

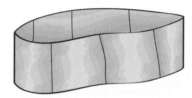

Step 3

4 Baste a line of stitches ½" from the top edge of the tier. Pull one thread to loosely gather. You will adjust the gathers later.

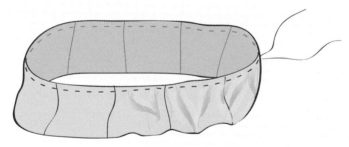

Step 4

5 Sew 12 squares into a circle to form the second tier. Press and topstitch each seam. Again, baste and gather the top edge of the tier, adjusting the gathers so that it is the same width as the bottom of the first tier.

6 Pin the gathered edge of the second tier to the ungathered bottom edge of the first tier. Stitch together and turn right side out. Press the seams toward the first tier and topstitch in place.

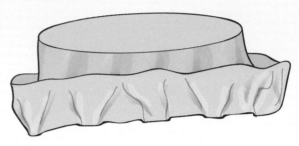

Step 6

7 Sew 16 squares into a circle to form the third tier. Press and topstitch each seam. Gather the top edge as you did with the previous tier.

8 Pin the gathered edge of the third tier to ungathered bottom edge of the second tier. Stitch together and turn right side out. Press and topstitch on the second tier side. If you are making a child's size 12/18m, 2y, or 3/4y, skip to Step 10. For all other sizes, continue with Step 9.

9 Sew 20 squares into a circle to form the fourth tier. Press and topstitch each seam. Gather in the same manner you did the previous tiers. Gather the fourth section so it is the same size as the straight edge of the third tier.

Creating the Waistband

10 Fuse the lightweight interfacing to the wrong side of your waistband pieces.

11 Take one of the waistband pieces and fold in half with short sides together. Mark the center and open the piece back up. Make two ½-inch buttonholes, 2" apart, each approximately 1" from the center. The buttonholes should start 1½" from the top edge of the waistband.

12 Hold the two waistband pieces with right sides together and stitch along the two short sides.

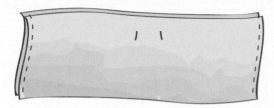

Step 12

13 Turn the top edge of the waistband over ¼" to the wrong side and press. Turn over 1" to the wrong side and press.

14 With the wrong side facing up, stitch along the bottom edge of the casing you've created. Stitch the entire casing closed.

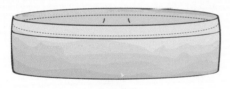

Step 14

Inserting the Drawstring

15 Create the drawstring by cutting 44" × 2" strips of fabric. Determine how long you want your drawstring to be by measuring your waist and adding approximately 30". For example, if your waist is 35", you will want a 65" strip of fabric, so you will need to sew two 44" sections right sides together and cut to fit.

16 Fold the strip wrong sides together and press. Open up and fold the raw edges to the inside and press. Fold again so the raw edges are enclosed and pin together.

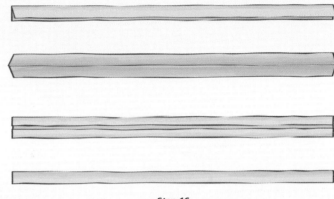

Step 16

17 Sew the folded edges together, tucking in the edges.

18 Feed the drawstring through one of the buttonholes by attaching a safety pin to one end. Feed the drawstring all the way through the casing, coming out the opposite buttonhole.

Finishing

19 Pin the gathered edge of the top tier to the edge of the waistband that doesn't have the drawstring, right sides together. Stitch together, turn right side out, and press.

20 Turn the bottom edge of the skirt under ½" and press. Turn another ½", press, and stitch.

21 Press the entire skirt and enjoy!

Upscaled Cardigan

Upscaled Cardigan

One blissful shopping trip with my sister to the thrift store yielded a small collection of adorable but slightly outdated cardigans. An idea was born, and off to the fabric collection I flew. What resulted was this adorable cardigan, perfect for spring, summer, or fall. I can't stop now—every sad-looking cardigan I find must come home with me to be given new life.

Supplies

1 button-down cardigan

Fabric-covered button kit (available in the notions section of fabric stores) in the same size as the buttons on the cardigan, and larger ones if desired for flower centers

Miscellaneous bits of fabric, enough to cover the buttons you choose

2 pieces of fabric for the sleeve ruffles:
Small cardigan: 4½" × 20"
Medium cardigan: 5½" × 22"
Large cardigan: 6½" × 24"
X-large cardigan: 6½" × 26"

Vellum or tracing paper

Wool felt pieces (approximately 15 pieces, each measuring 1" × 2")

Miscellaneous buttons and trims (optional)

Note: Cut the sleeve ruffles ½" wider (5", 6", 7", 7") if you are not using a serger.

Prep

1 Put the cardigan on and make a light pencil mark around each sleeve where it reaches your elbow. Remove the cardigan and make a straight cut to remove the bottom half of each sleeve. Remove the buttons from the cardigan.

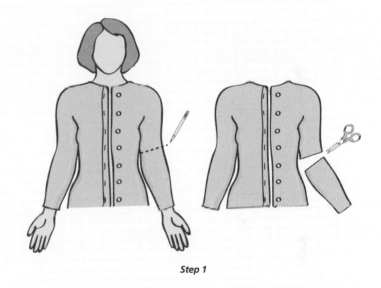

Step 1

Creating the Sleeves

2 Cut two sleeve ruffle pieces to the measurements given at left. Sew each into a circle by holding the two short ends of one piece with right sides and stitching along the short end.

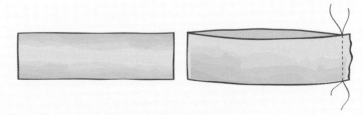

Step 2

3 Hem the edge of your ruffle. I prefer to do a rolled hem on a serger, but if you don't have one, you can cut the hem of the sleeve ½" longer. Fold the hem to the wrong side ¼" and press. Fold the hem ¼" more, press, and stitch.

4 Gather the unfinished edge of the ruffle by sewing a loose running stitch on your sewing machine and pulling one of the threads to gather. Gather it to approximately half the original size.

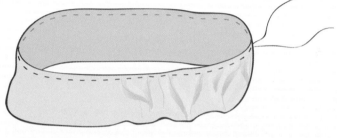

Step 4

5 With right sides together, line up the gathered edge of the ruffle and the raw edge of the cardigan sleeve. Stitch together and serge, if you have a serger. Turn right side out, press, and topstitch along the sweater.

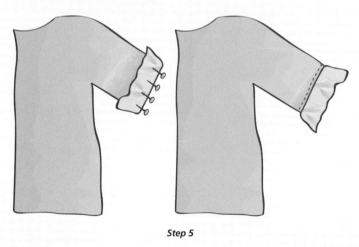

Step 5

Finishing

6 Using your spare bits of fabric and following the directions on the kit, cover your buttons in fabric. Sew the smaller buttons in place on the cardigan in the same spots you removed them. Save the larger buttons for Step 7.

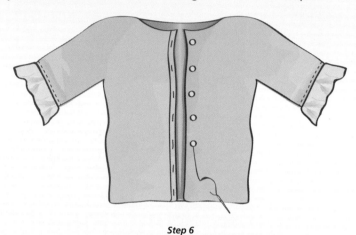

Step 6

7 Using vellum or tracing paper, copy the pattern pieces on page 163 and cut out the petal shapes out of wool felt. Arrange them in a flower-shaped cluster along the upper left chest near the shoulder and stitch in place. Sew one of the larger fabric-covered buttons in the center of your flower shape. Place as many flowers as you would like.

Step 7

8 Adorn the cardigan with other buttons or trims as you desire.

Ruffled Head Scarf

Ruffled Head Scarf

When I first thought of this project, I envisioned lazy afternoons in the garden, wearing the scarf to keep the sun off of my hair. (Your skin isn't the only thing you need to protect!) I'm so happy with how it turned out—it embodies more of a lifestyle to me than just a regular scarf. Imagine seeing a content gardener at work. You can tell her head scarf is handmade, and she is harvesting vegetables for that night's dinner. I wanted to capture that simple, slow-paced lifestyle with this project. A tall order for a simple scarf? Maybe, but I think it hit the mark. This pattern makes two adult scarves, four children's scarves, or one adult and two children's scarves. Keep several on hand for gifts!

Supplies

49 fabric scraps, each cut to 3" square
1 piece of fabric for the lining, 17" × 17"
1 strip of fabric for the ruffle (per scarf), 2" × 44"
1 package of double-fold bias tape

Prep

1 Make sure that all of your fabric pieces are either washed or unwashed. As these may be the remnants of several different projects, the pre-care for those fabrics may have varied depending on the project.

Creating the Patchwork

2 Sew seven squares together into a strip, using a ¼" seam allowance. Press the seams open and topstitch ⅛" from each seam to finish the edges.

Step 2

3 Repeat Step 2 with the other squares to create six more strips for a total of seven strips.

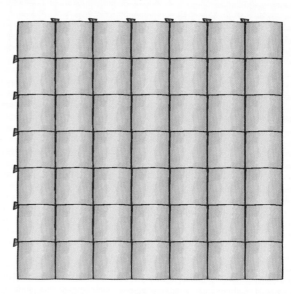

Step 3

4 Sew the long sides of the strips together to create a patchwork piece. Press the seams open and topstitch ⅛" from each seam to finish the edges.

5 Lay the patchwork piece on top of the lining. Cut both pieces in half diagonally. You now have the pieces for two adult-sized head scarves. If you wish to make child-sized scarves, cut the adult-sized triangle in half (indicated by the dotted line in the illustration).

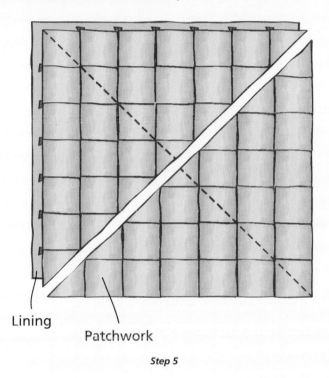

Lining

Patchwork

Step 5

Making the Ruffle Strip

6 Fold the strip for the ruffle in half lengthwise with wrong sides together. Press. Sew a loose running stitch along the raw edges and gather loosely by pulling one thread.

7 With the right side of the patchwork scarf facing up, pin the ruffle to the two short sides of the scarf, with the raw edges of fabric touching, and the finished edge of the ruffle overlapping the patchwork by at least 1". Stay-stitch the ruffle strip in place. The adult head scarf will take the full ruffle strip; you will want to shorten the ruffle on the child-sized scarf.

8 Place the lining right side down on top of the patchwork piece, sandwiching the ruffle in between. Sew the lining and patchwork piece together, leaving the long straight edge open. Trim the corners; turn right side out. Press and topstitch the head scarf along the ruffled edges.

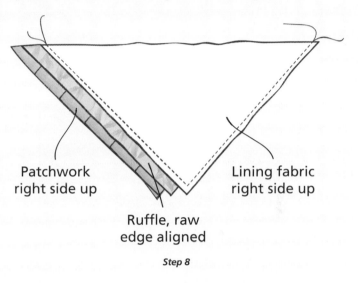

Patchwork right side up

Lining fabric right side up

Ruffle, raw edge aligned

Step 8

Finishing

9 Unfold the slightly wider side of the bias tape and pin it to the long unfinished edge of the head scarf on the lining side. Leave 12" tails on each side for adults, 9" tails on each side for children. Stay-stitch the bias tape to the head scarf along the crease of the fold.

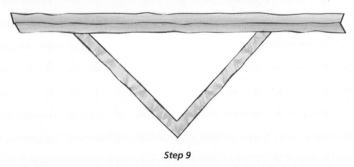

Step 9

10 Turn the bias tape to the right side of the head scarf and topstitch along the entire tape, tucking the ends inside. Press.

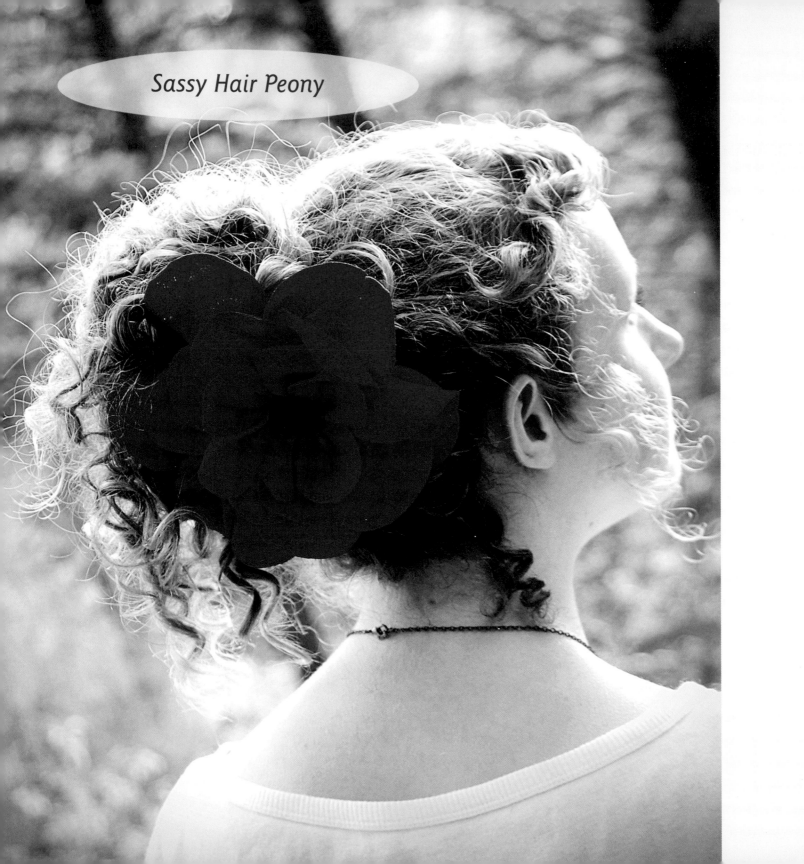

Sassy Hair Peony

Sassy Hair Peony

This flower is toting the name "sassy" because at about 6 inches wide, it isn't for the bashful or faint of heart! It makes a big statement, and pairs equally well with a cotton tee shirt or an elegant black dress. I used the remnants of a vintage organza dress for this flower, but quilting cottons would be lovely, too. Try incorporating a cotton version with a pin back into the Upscaled Cardigan on page 145.

Supplies

Vellum or tracing paper
20 pieces of fabric for large petals, each 3½" × 4"
16 pieces of fabric for medium petals, each 3" × 3"
12 pieces of fabric for small petals, each 2½" × 2½"
Spray starch
1 button, 1" diameter (try fabric-covered buttons)
Hot glue gun
1 alligator clip
Small piece of wool felt in a coordinating color

Prep

1 Using vellum or tracing paper, copy the pattern pieces on page 161 and cut out all the petal pieces.

Creating the Petals

2 Hold two petal pieces of the same size with right sides together and sew around the curved edges of the petal, leaving the flat bottom edge open. Clip curved seam allowances so the petals will lay flat. Turn right side out. Spray lightly with spray starch and press on a low setting. Repeat with all the petal pieces.

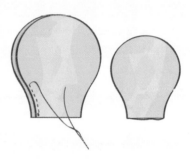

Step 2

Joining the Petals

3 With a needle and thread, sew across the flat edges of all the large petals with continuous stitching. When all ten petals are on the strand, pull the thread so the petals gather together in the center.

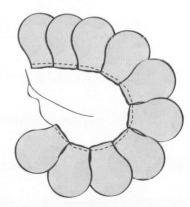

Step 3

4 Reinforce with stitches in the center. Repeat with the medium petals and then with the small petals.

Step 4

Layering the Petal Sections

5 Place the small petal section on top of the medium petal section and stitch together at the center.

Step 5

6 Place the large petal section underneath the medium petal section and sew all three pieces together in the center. Sew a button in the center of the small petal section.

Step 6

Finishing

7 Using a hot glue gun, attach the back of the flower to the top side of the alligator clip. Make sure not to glue the clip shut! I like to attach the clip to a wooden dowel or pencil before applying the glue.

Step 7

8 Cut a small rounded square out of wool felt and glue it over the top inside of the alligator clip.

Step 8

Tattered Rose Headband

Tattered Rose Headband

This headband is the perfect combination of elegant and rustic. Luscious silk dupioni is torn and sculpted back together into tight roses and then attached to an equally chic headband. Or try attaching them to bobby pins. The shabby roses would also be gorgeous as an embellishment on a bag or garment. When tearing silk, use your scissors and snip one end of the selvedge about one inch. Rip quickly. I usually discard the first piece, which tends to be uneven. Snip the selvedge again and create your tears. Silk will give off a lot of loose strands; don't worry about cutting them off—they add to the shabby look of the flowers in this project.

Supplies

1 torn strip of silk for the small rose, 1" × 15"
1 torn strip of silk for the medium rose, 1" × 20"
1 torn strip of silk for the large rose, 1" × 25"
Vellum or tracing paper
1 square of wool felt for the base of the flowers, 3" × 3"
5" length of lingerie elastic (elastic that has a decorative edge; it comes in many colors)
2 pieces of silk for the headband, each 2½" × 18"
2 torn strips of silk for covering the seams of the headband, each 1" × 3"

Forming the Roses

1 Thread your needle and anchor your thread at one end of a torn silk strip with a knot. Roll the end of your silk a few times and sew a few stitches to create a nub that will become the center of your rose.

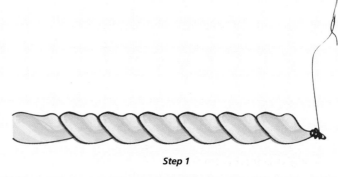

Step 1

2 Twist the first 6" of the silk strip. Wrap the twisted silk around the center nub one time. Whip-stitch underneath to hold the wrapped section in place.

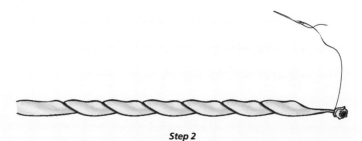

Step 2

3 Continue twisting the silk, about 6" at a time, wrapping it around the center and whip-stitching it in place to form the rose, until your length of silk is gone. Tuck the end of the silk strip under the bottom of the flower and stitch it in place. Repeat Steps 2 and 3 with the other silk strips to form the other two roses.

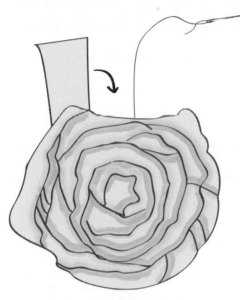

Step 3

4 Using vellum or tracing paper, copy the circle base on page 172 and cut it out of wool felt. Arrange the roses on it in a cluster, overlapping the edges a bit. Pin the roses in place and sew the bottoms of the roses to the felt with hidden stitches.

Step 4

Forming the Headband

5 Fold one of the headband pieces in half lengthwise with right sides together. Stitch the raw edges together along the length of the band. Turn right side out using a wooden dowel or a turning tool. Press with a cool iron, with the seam centered at the back. Make the second headband piece the same way.

Note: Look for turning tools in the tools section of the fabric store.

Step 5

6 Place one end of each headband section on top of the other, at a slight angle. Baste together. Repeat with the other side, being careful not to twist the pieces.

Step 6

7 With the headbands seam side down, place one end of the headband on top of the elastic so they overlap by ½". Sew securely in place. Repeat with the opposite ends of the headband and elastic.

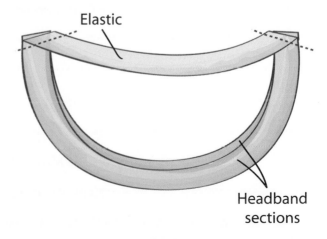

Elastic

Headband sections

Step 7

8 With a needle and thread, secure one end of your 3" torn strip to the wrong side where the headband and the elastic meet. Wrap the silk strip around the seam two or three times. Trim the strip, tuck under the edge, and stitch in place. Repeat with the opposite side of the headband.

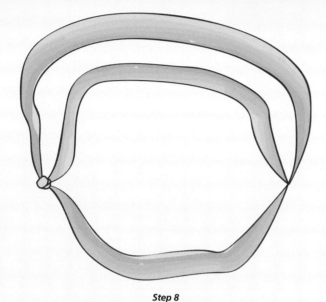

Step 8

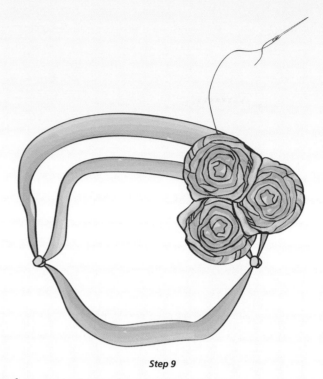

Step 9

Note: Remember that silk cannot be washed—please dry-clean only!

9 Try on the headband and determine where you want your rose cluster to go. Mark the spot with pins and remove the headband. Lay the headband on a flat surface and place the wool felt circle holding your roses in the marked spot. Pin in place and use invisible stitches underneath to secure.

Pattern Pieces

Fruit Appliqué Tablecloth and Fruit Magnets

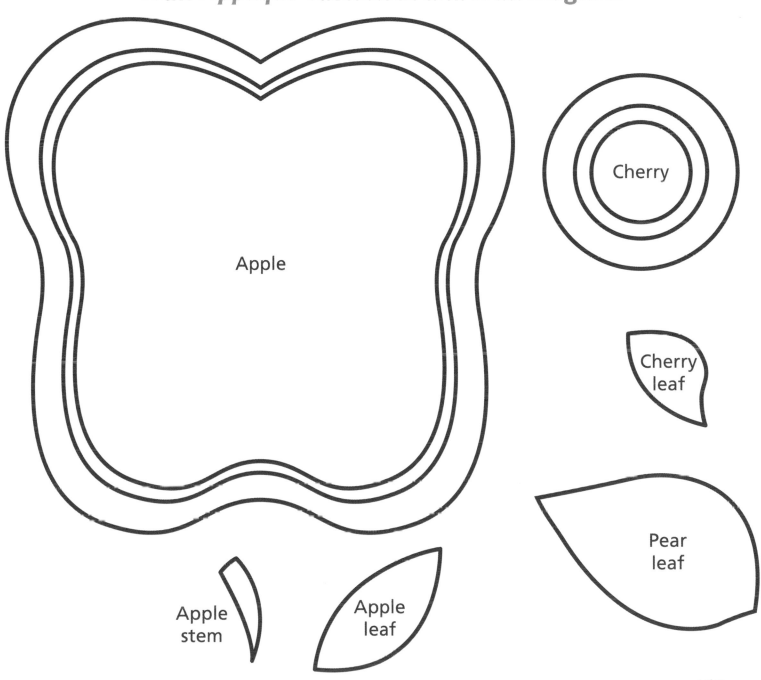

Apple

Cherry

Cherry leaf

Pear leaf

Apple stem

Apple leaf

Fruit Appliqué Tablecloth and Fruit Magnets

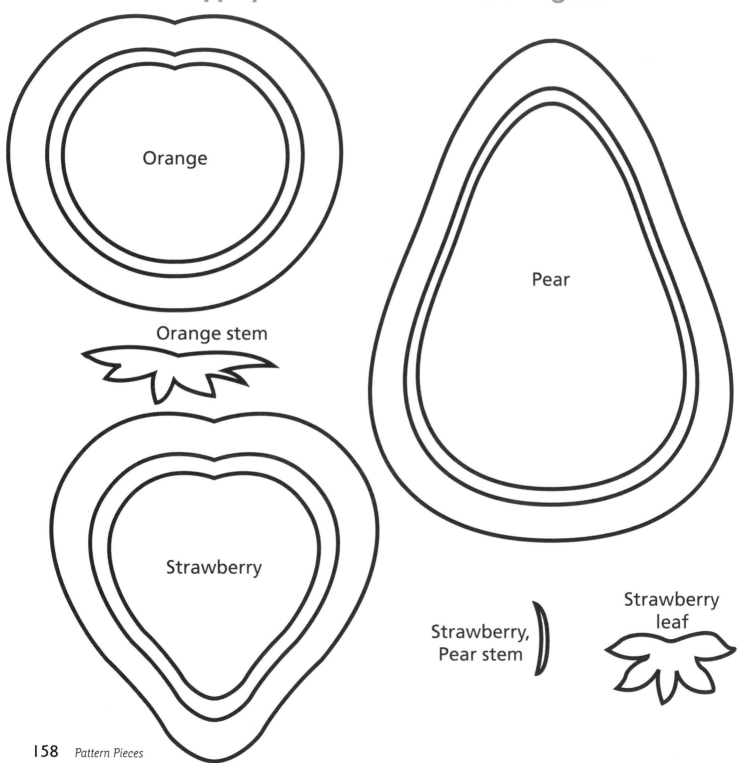

Orange

Orange stem

Pear

Strawberry

Strawberry, Pear stem

Strawberry leaf

Sweet Treats Towels

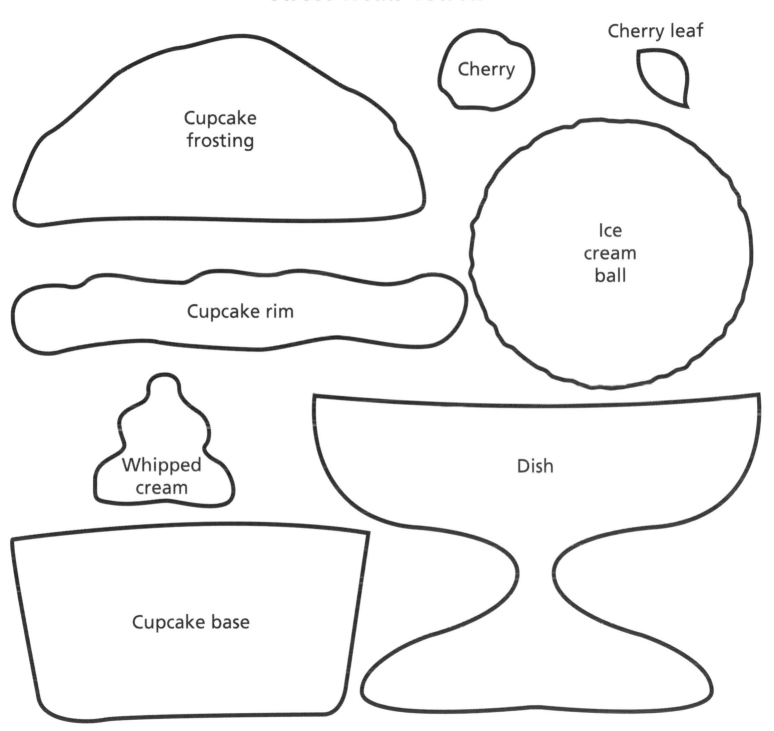

Cupcake frosting

Cherry

Cherry leaf

Ice cream ball

Cupcake rim

Whipped cream

Dish

Cupcake base

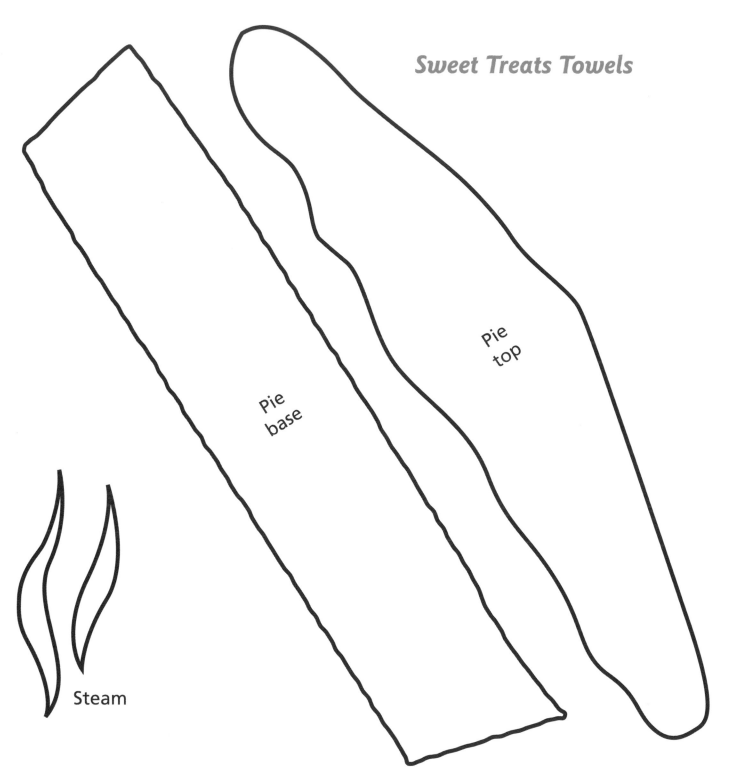

Sweet Treats Towels

Pie top

Pie base

Steam

Herbal Sachet

Daisy
center

Lavender
petals

Daisy petals

Garden Pillows

Leaves

Mum
petals

Sassy Hair Peony

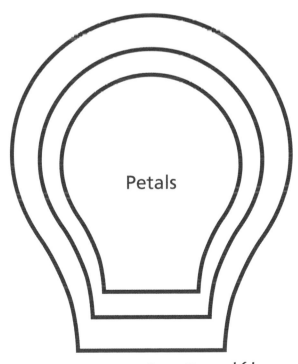

Petals

Bubbly Shower Curtain

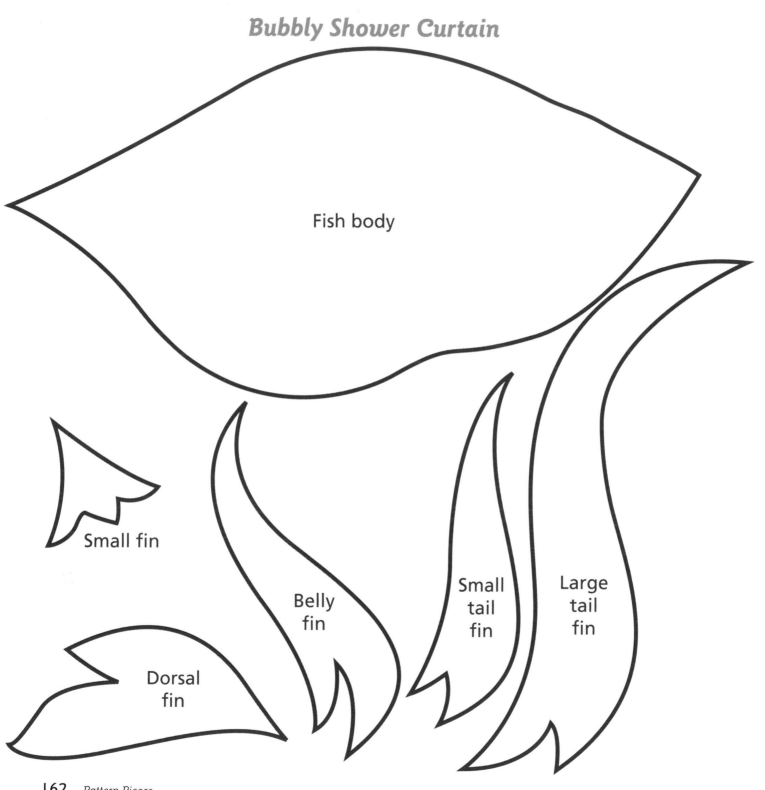

Fish body

Small fin

Dorsal fin

Belly fin

Small tail fin

Large tail fin

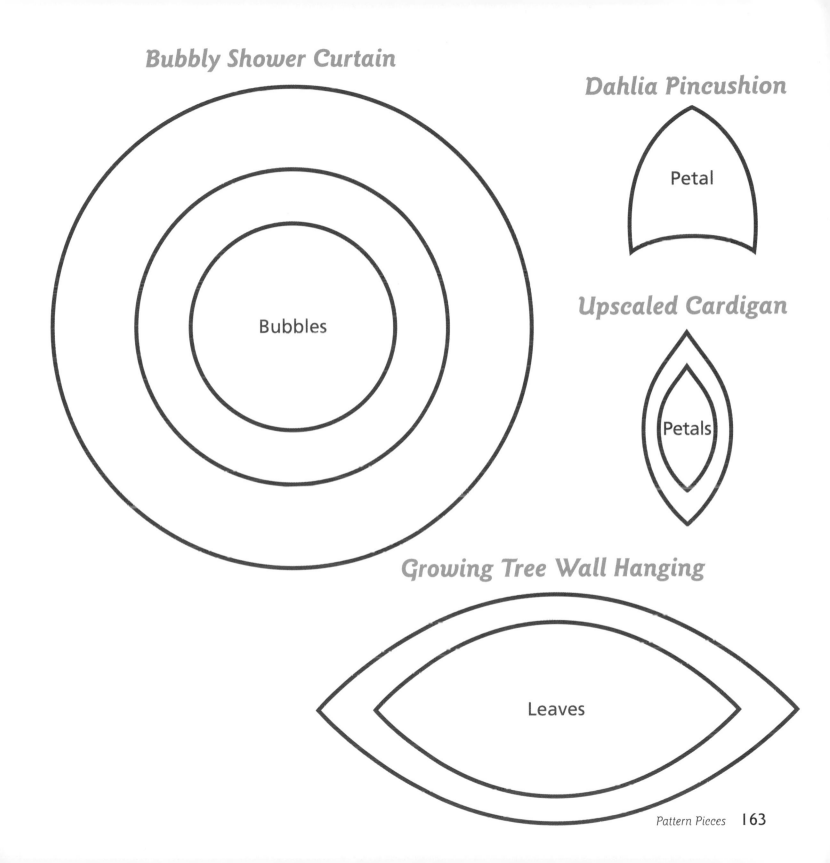

Bubbly Shower Curtain

Bubbles

Dahlia Pincushion

Petal

Upscaled Cardigan

Petals

Growing Tree Wall Hanging

Leaves

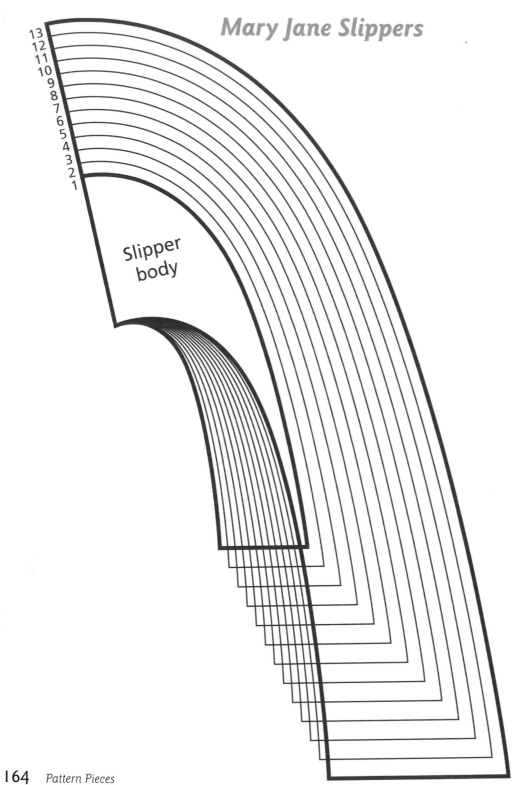

Mary Jane Slippers

13
12
11
10
9
8
7
6
5
4
3
2
1

Slipper
body

Mary Jane Slippers

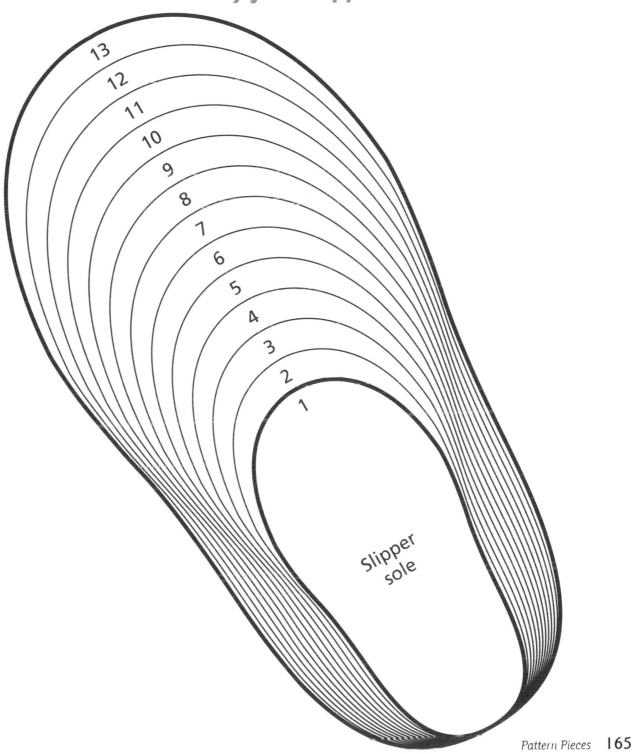

13
12
11
10
9
8
7
6
5
4
3
2
1

Slipper
sole

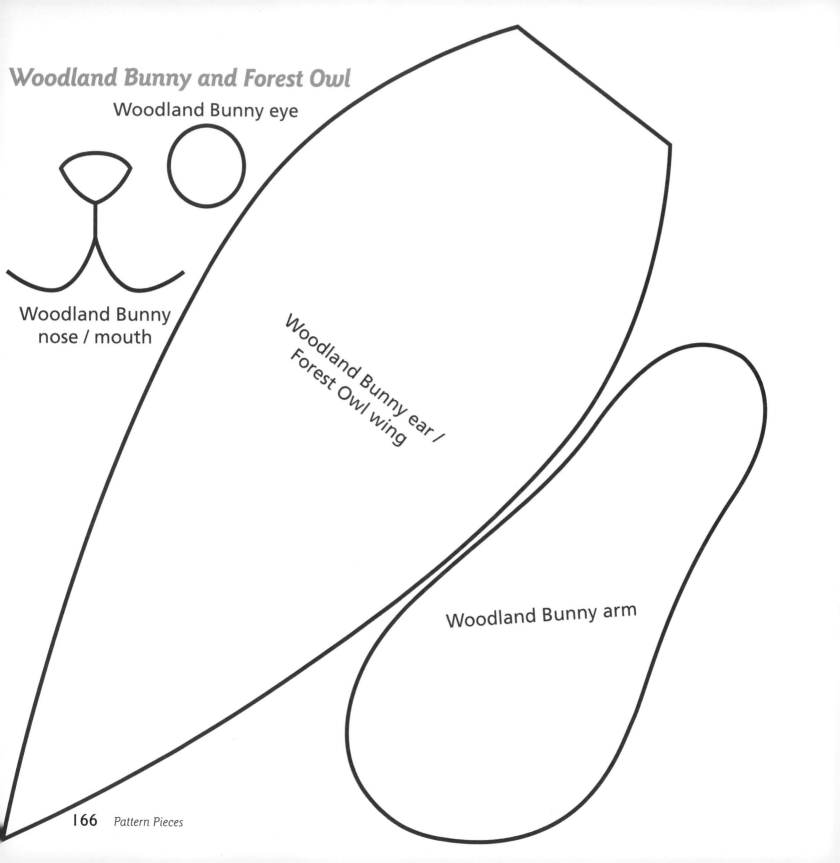

Woodland Bunny and Forest Owl

Woodland Bunny eye

Woodland Bunny
nose / mouth

Woodland Bunny ear /
Forest Owl wing

Woodland Bunny arm

Woodland Bunny and Forest Owl

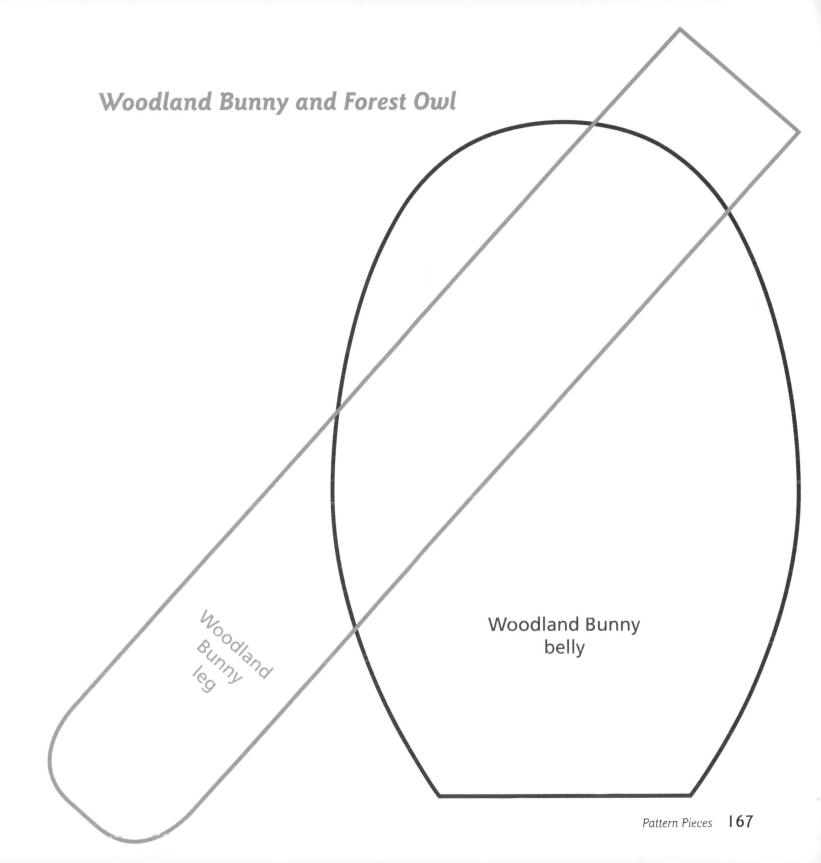

Woodland Bunny leg

Woodland Bunny belly

Woodland Bunny and Forest Owl

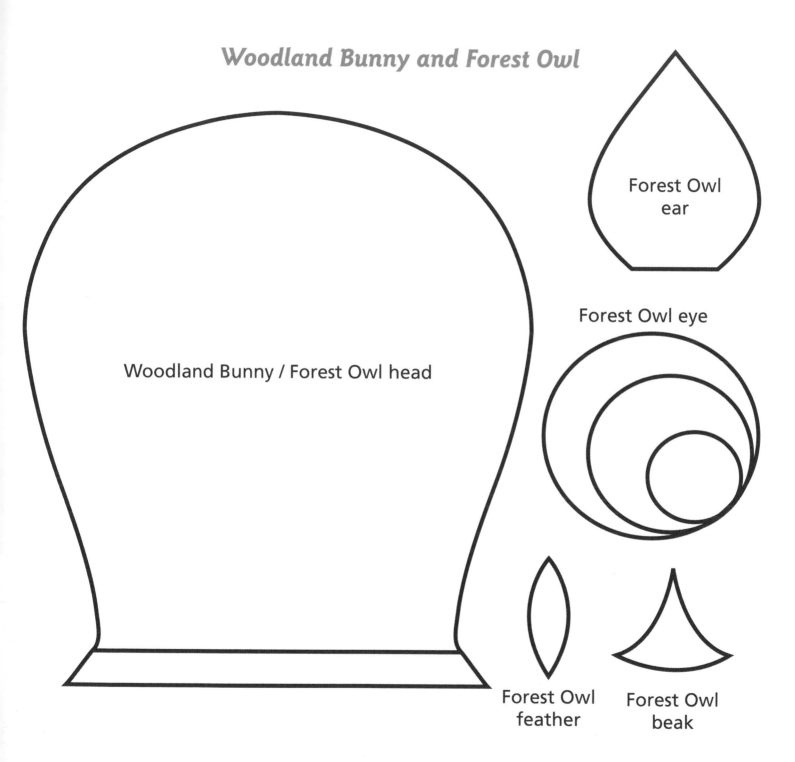

Forest Owl ear

Woodland Bunny / Forest Owl head

Forest Owl eye

Forest Owl feather

Forest Owl beak

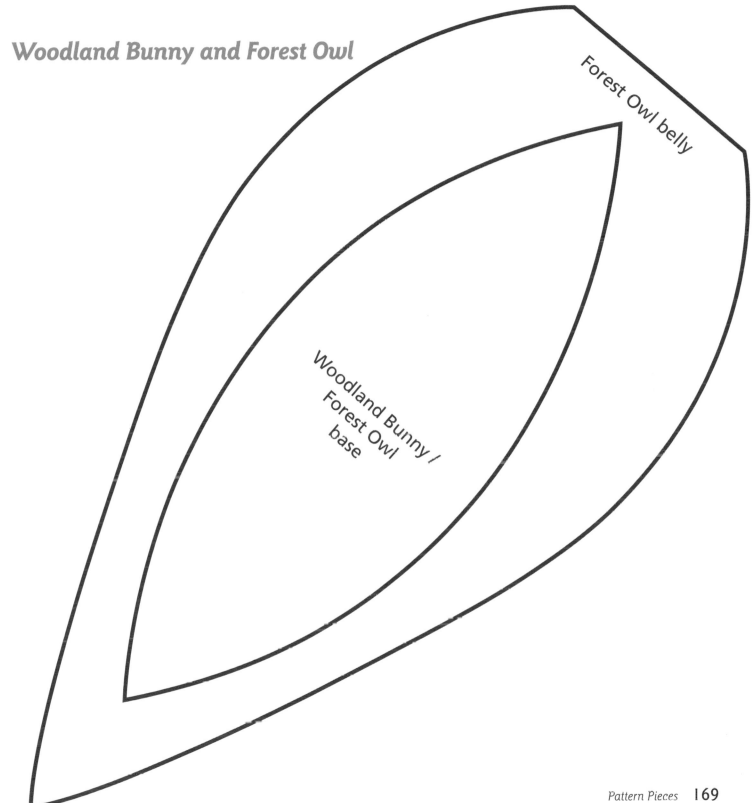

Woodland Bunny and Forest Owl

Forest Owl belly

Woodland Bunny /
Forest Owl
base

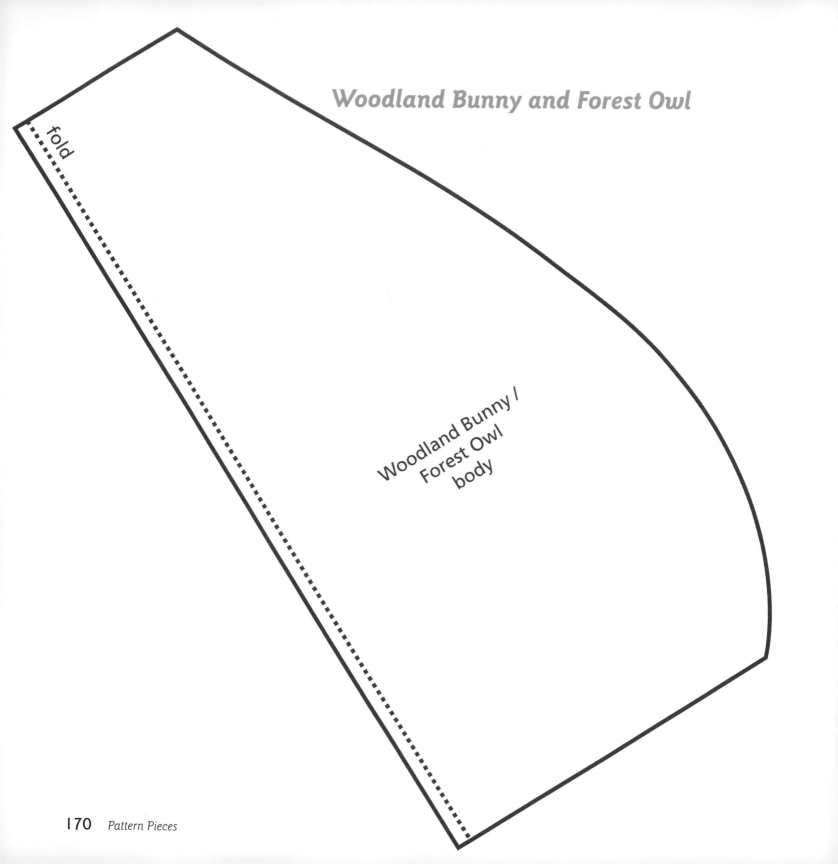

Woodland Bunny and Forest Owl

fold

Woodland Bunny /
Forest Owl
body

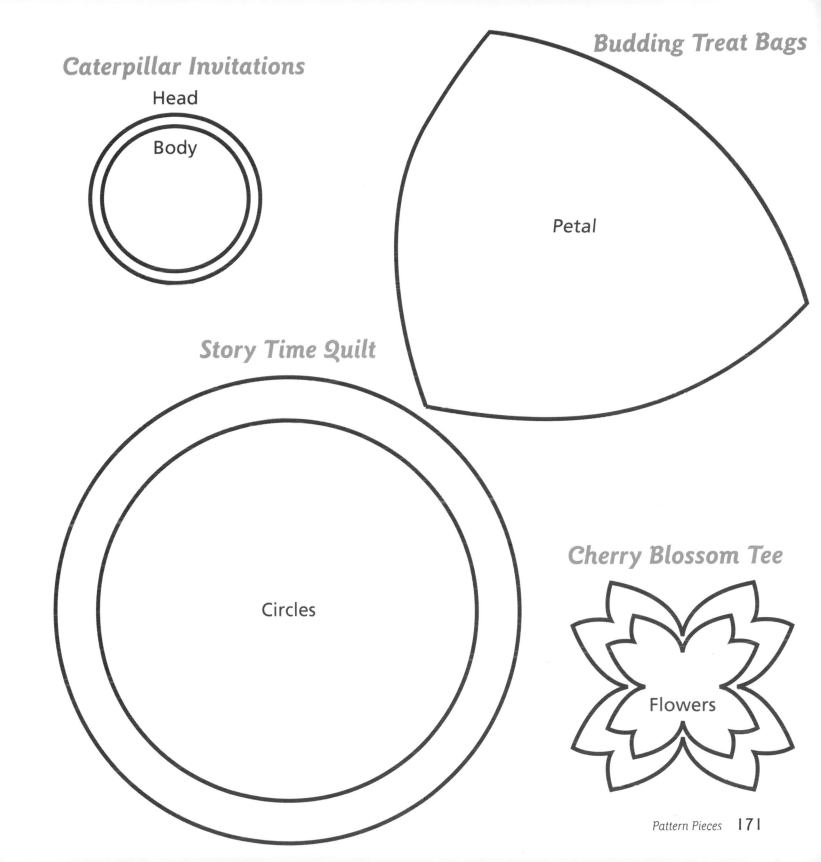

Caterpillar Invitations

Head

Body

Budding Treat Bags

Petal

Story Time Quilt

Circles

Cherry Blossom Tee

Flowers

Birthday Party Garland

Butterfly Pin

Outer wings

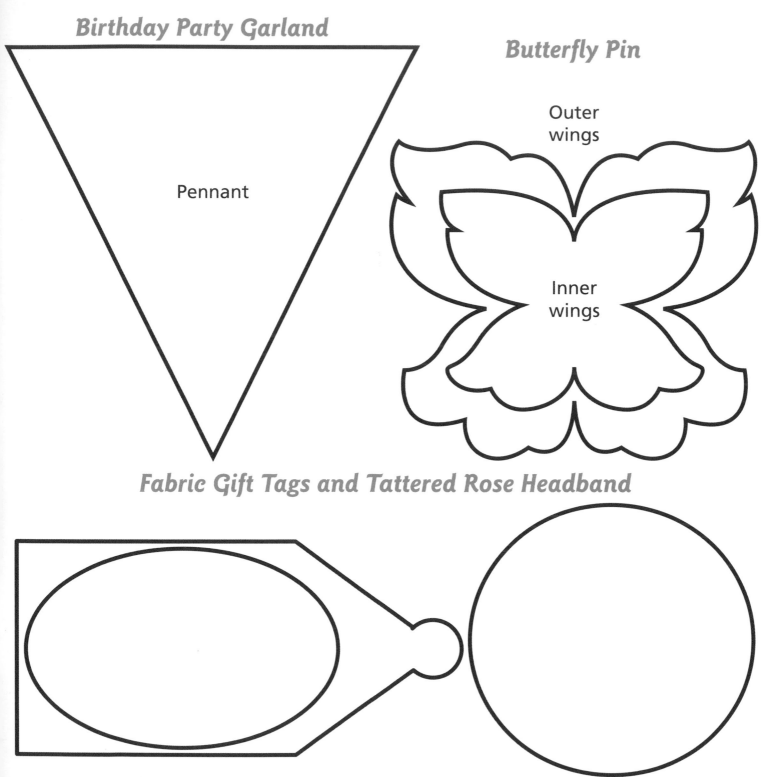

Pennant

Inner wings

Fabric Gift Tags and Tattered Rose Headband

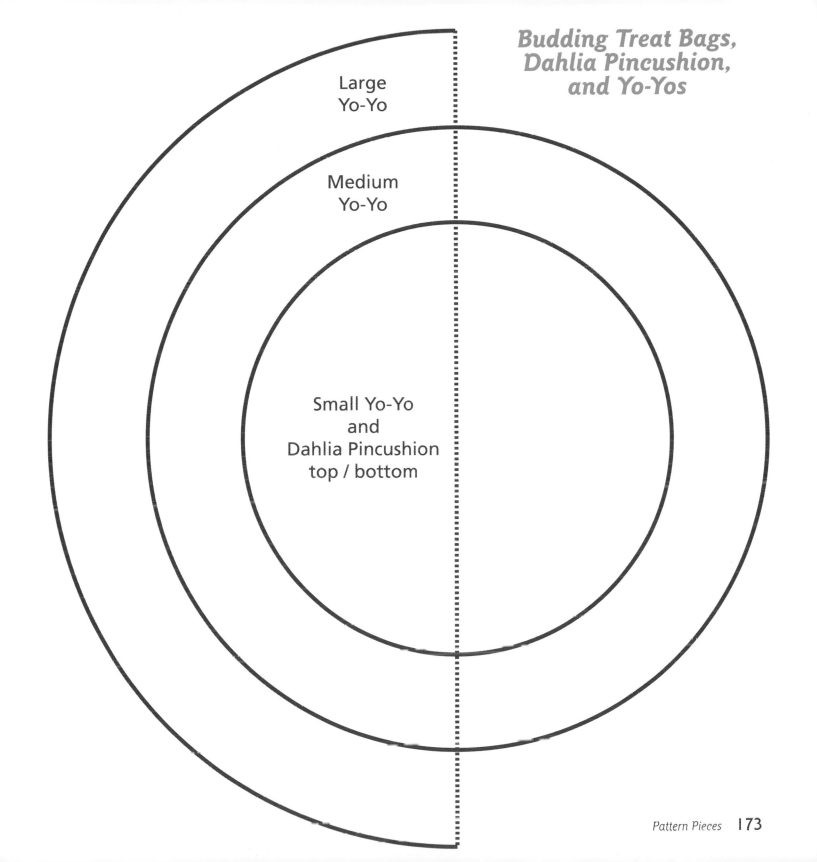

Large
Yo-Yo

Medium
Yo-Yo

Small Yo-Yo
and
Dahlia Pincushion
top / bottom

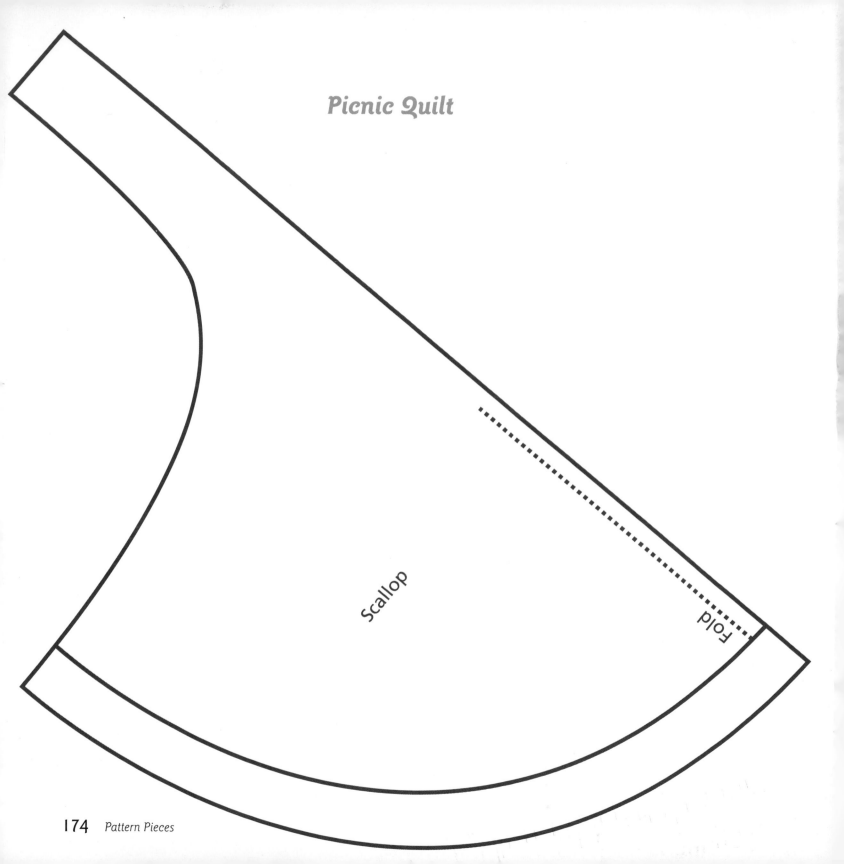

Picnic Quilt

Scallop

Fold